A

Do not be afraid!

Above All, Love

DISCERNING WAYS TO DEFEND LIFE
WITH CHARITY AND JUSTICE

Elizabeth Gillette

Our Sunday Visitor
Huntington, Indiana

Our Sunday Visitor Publishing Division
Our Sunday Visitor, Inc.
200 Noll Plaza
Huntington, IN 46750
www.osv.com
1-800-348-2440

ISBN: 978-1-63966-034-6 (Inventory No. T2786)
1. RELIGION—Christian Living—Social Issues.
2. RELIGION—Christian Living—Spiritual Growth.
3. RELIGION—Christianity—Catholic.
eISBN: 978-1-63966-035-3
LCCN: 2023936649

Cover design: Tyler Ottinger
Cover art: Adobestock
Interior design: Amanda Falk

PRINTED IN THE UNITED STATES OF AMERICA

*Dedicated with love, profound longing,
and hope in Christ Jesus,
to my lost son, Michael Joseph.
I allowed fear to rip you from me
before your birth.
May the sorrow of our parting always
remind me and encourage me
to love above all else.
May your life have meaning,
no matter how short it was.
May we meet again in heaven.
P.S. Dad, I love you.
Try hard, critique, adjust, try again.*

Contents

Introduction

A few years after my abortion, I was sitting with my oldest brother in the grass overlooking the farm fields where we grew up. At the time, my brother was not aware of what I had done to my first child. Our state had just adopted a sweeping new measure that allowed adults to purchase "Plan B," otherwise known as the morning after pill, without a prescription. We began to discuss this measure, and our conversation turned to abortion. My brother looked at me and said, "How can anyone *do that*?"

I shook my head and shrugged, nestling deeper into the secrecy of my abortion. At least I could outwardly pretend I was innocent of the death of my child. But on the inside, I was dying, longing to be free of the secret, to find healing from the abortion that had changed me so violently. How *could I* have done that? How did it happen? I had always believed abortion was wrong, but in the heart of the crisis, I was unable to summon the courage I needed to face an unplanned pregnancy. My boyfriend insisted he was too young to be a father and made an appointment at an abortion facility for me. He drove me there and was relieved when I swallowed the pill that ended our child's life. I kept my pregnancy and my abortion a secret from my family, friends, and church community. I was terrified they would reject me, call me a murderer, or be disgusted with me. I had crossed the line and gone to the other side, the side that kills babies in the womb, and I was afraid they would never forgive me for killing my unborn child.

Where were the pro-life warriors? Where were the compassionate voices of reason telling me I was capable enough to be a mother? Where was the strength of my boyfriend, the father of this child? Even he hadn't loved me enough to protect me, or our baby, from abortion.

There were no prayer warriors outside of the abortion facility when I arrived the day of my appointment. There were no alternatives or options counseled to me at the facility. No crisis pregnancy centers nearby, no hope. I felt completely alone. I felt betrayed by the man who was supposed to love me. I felt abandoned by everything and everyone.

And then, I let fear steal my child from me.

After my abortion, I found myself wedged between two polarized sides. The pro-choice narrative told me I had nothing to grieve, and I was betraying the rights of women for regretting my abortion. The pro-life narrative hurled condemnation at me for what I had done. I was trapped in a valley of deep sadness, unable to heal, unable to move on.

As the years passed and I became a mother again, I began to participate in the pro-life mission. I wanted to be truly pro-life, to stand up for those who could not fight, and to do so in tangible ways. I went to rallies, prayed outside of clinics, testified in court cases, and helped promote laws limiting abortion funding by the state. I even surrendered the secret of my abortion publicly with a viral video and returned to the Church through the Sacrament of Reconciliation. But the more deeply I became involved in the ministry, the more fractures I could see within it, fractures that hindered the goal of saving unborn children and supporting their mothers.

Those who oppose the pro-life mission often refer to those involved as bigoted and selfish, not caring about individual people, personal choice, or freedom. They say we do not care about children and mothers after the child is born, or that we're cruel toward women who have been raped. They call us hateful, judgmental, callous, and insensitive. While our hearts may not be any of these things, we face this stigma with every step we take in our ministry. Why?

Sadly, the pro-life ministry has become fractured by discord and divisions. The goal to save lives is obstructed by our own misdeeds, shortcomings, and misunderstandings. Arguments over how best to reach women stir up conflict. Anger on sidewalks outside of clinics pushes women toward the decision to have an abortion. Fingers pointed at broken women keep them from accepting our help. A lack of awareness of our community pro-life organizations keeps us from working together. I realized that many pro-life warriors spend too much time worrying about the wrong things, and not enough time loving the vulnerable women and unborn children who need our help. Like me, have you become frustrated with dissension, hatred, or rash judgment among people who claim to be pro-life? Do you long for unity between all those who work toward the end of abortion? Do you lash out when pro-abortion individuals ridicule you, or grieve when others lash out in the name of defending life? Are you looking for a deeper, more tangible way to say yes to God's call for your own pro-life efforts or ministry? Are you ready to do the hard work to become a more mature and spiritually equipped pro-life warrior? Do you wonder if you have made mistakes in seeking to defend life, but you don't know where or how? Do you long for a blueprint to guide you as you embark more fully into the calling you have heard from God?

I truly believe the first step to healing the fractures among those who are pro-life is for all of us to look inward and strive for sanctification. This is true whether we are actively involved in pro-life ministry or merely supporting the pro-life mission in any way we can. Becoming a saint is not an easy task. We strive to live the best we can while being pulled in a thousand directions. Children, spouses, work, school, play, and countless other tasks, commitments, and activities make it hard to take the time we need to learn more about God and grow in our relationship with him.

This book is meant to help you delve deeply into the word of God, to peel back the layers of your own life and step closer to sanctification. This book is for any Catholic who longs to engage in pro-life work with compassion, care, and love in a world where life is not valued, and where rash judgment abounds. In this book, you will reflect on your own pro-life efforts, discovering what the word of God and the *Catechism of the Catholic Church* teach about reaching others both within and outside the Faith. You will explore ways to interact as Jesus did: with love, compassion, gentle truth, and forgiveness. By reshaping your own thoughts, attitudes, and actions, you will be better equipped to love those who have been traumatized by abortion, challenge those who stand against the truth, and say yes to God's call to love and fight for innocent life, as he did and does.

Be courageous as you learn to challenge the detrimental attitudes, rash judgments, and fractures that often impede our pro-life efforts. Stand firm while cultivating a mind, body, and spirit full of empathy, compassion, and love for those traumatized by abortion or still enslaved to the sin of abortion.

HOW TO USE THIS BOOK

You have in your hands a book with which to self-reflect and grow. This book will not try to persuade you that abortion is wrong, nor will it equip you with specific arguments to persuade others of the same. Instead, this book will take you deep into the realm of your own spirit, where you will pray, reflect, and encounter Christ. As faithful Catholics, we have a beautiful and sound base of knowledge to guide us in our pro-life mission. During your reflection, you will discover what the word of God, the *Catechism*, and some of the saints teach regarding the virtues, attitudes, behaviors, and dispositions necessary to cooperate fully with God's will while seeking to defend life.

This study is primarily meant to facilitate a personal conversation between you and God, but it is also possible to use it in a group setting.

You will need your Bible, your *Catechism*, and a pen while you journey through this book.

Throughout the book, you will find spaces to write your thoughts or answers to questions posed. Feel free to write directly in this book. You may also want a journal, as certain topics may entice you into deep thought. You may become defensive, angry, or annoyed. It is never easy to look inward at our own shortcomings, or to stretch ourselves beyond comfort while we grow and mature toward holiness. If you find yourself reacting in cynical or defensive ways to any topic, take the time to pray about it. Ask the Holy Spirit to shed light on the issue.

At the end of the book, you will find an examination of conscience. This examination will walk you through insightful questions, taking a deeper look at your own thoughts, words, actions, and deeds, as well as how the Lord might be calling you to conversion in your pro-life work.

My goal for each of you who reads this book is that you will become more like Christ in your ministry, able to spread God's life-giving love through your thoughts, words, and actions to all those you encounter. My hope is that you will feel equipped to minister effectively to women, their unborn children, and all who have been affected by abortion, including pro-abortion advocates we encounter.

Be courageous and bold as you journey inward so that you can venture outward, to be able to stand in the gap between the culture of death and those ravaged by abortion.

ONE

Standing in the Gap

Come and take them.
— King Leonidas of Sparta

Leonidas, king of Sparta, stood in the gap between two mountains with an army of three hundred heroic Spartan soldiers to keep King Xerxes of Persia from taking free Greece. Before the first day of battle, King Xerxes wrote to Leonidas demanding that he give up his weapons. Leonidas simply wrote back, "Come and take them."

The Spartans were incredibly disciplined and fought as a group, working together for one purpose. As the battle raged against the Persian army's advance, the Spartans used their round shields to create a phalanx formation. They held their shields together tightly, like a turtle shell. Soldiers behind the front of the formation used long spears to stab outward, making the formation extremely deadly. If anyone fell in battle, another Spartan would "stand in the gap" and continue to fight.

King Leonidas lost this battle, but he marked the beginning of the end for the Persian invasion, and Xerxes failed in his attempt to conquer the free people of Greece. Leonidas is remembered as a hero.

Today, standing in the gap is an idiom that describes the act of exposing oneself to danger in order to protect another. It is also used to describe taking the place of one who has fallen or cannot continue the fight.

We, as pro-life Catholics, must stand in the gap between the pro-choice culture of death and every innocent unborn child. We must stand in the gap to defend the post-abortive woman from the narrative that tells her she has no right to mourn and nothing to heal from, and from those who would judge her for her past choices. We must stand in the gap to defend every victim, woman or child, against Satan's wiles.

A beautiful example of a Catholic who stood in the gap to save her unborn child is St. Gianna Beretta Molla. Gianna was a laywoman who sacrificed her own life for that of her unborn child in 1962. She once said, "Love is the most beautiful sentiment the Lord has put into the souls of men and women." Gianna was a pediatrician and knew that "the doctor should not meddle. The right of the child to live is equal to the right of the mother's life. The doctor cannot decide; it is a sin to kill in the womb."

Gianna was diagnosed with a fibroid tumor of the uterus when her pregnancy was just two months along. She was given several treatment options, including a hysterectomy. With great love, she chose the higher risk treatment to save her baby, knowing she might not survive. Her daughter was born healthy via cesarean section, but Gianna died of septic peritonitis, an infection of the lining of the abdomen, just seven days later. Gianna's example to choose the life of her unborn child over her own is an incredible testament to the responsibility we each have in this ministry: to lay down our lives for others (see Jn 15:13). Gianna gave her physical life for her child, choosing to carry her daughter and refuse medical treatments that would harm her baby. Gianna's example is the ultimate imitation of Christ's love. She was a true defender of life. She stood directly in the gap between life and death for her child and defied the advice of her doctors, who recommended her pregnancy be terminated to save her own life. What strength!

We may not be required to give our physical lives to save the unborn, but we must love as deeply as if we were.

REFLECTION

In the Old Testament book of Ezekiel, the Lord seeks a righteous person who will stand in the breach, or gap, and keep him from destroying the land. Read the passage below. How does this passage relate to our culture today?

> Thus I have searched among them for someone who would build a wall or stand in the breach before me to keep me from destroying the land; but I found no one. (Ezekiel 22:30)

Are you currently "standing in the gap" in any way (whether related to pro-life work or not) in your ministry, family, or life? Describe how. How does it make you feel? What are the benefits and drawbacks of standing in the gap? Do you feel properly equipped to stand in the gap in this way?

_____

_____

_____

_____

_____

_____

_____

Read the following Bible passage. How does this passage relate to the idiom "stand in the gap"? How did Jesus stand in the gap for all of us when he died on the cross?

This is my commandment: love one another as I love you. No one has greater love than this, to lay down one's life for one's friends. (John 15:12–13)

_____

_____

_____

_____

_____

_____

_____

Imagine King Leonidas of Sparta standing between innocent life and a world that destroys children in the womb. His weapons are drawn, and he is ready to fight to the death to protect. Now reread his one-line response to King Xerxes: "Come and take them!" What image does this create in your mind? What emotion does this evoke?

_____

_____

_____

_____

_____

_____

_____

_____

TWO

Answering the Call

Have patience with all things, but chiefly have
patience with yourself. Do not lose courage
in considering your own imperfections
but instantly set about remedying them
— every day begin the task anew.
— St. Francis de Sales

Working in pro-life ministry is an important calling, and one that we all receive in some form. It is challenging, riddled with uncertainty, but it can also be full of life, community, hope, reconciliation, and joy. Before we rush out into the world and say yes to pro-life ministry, we first need to recognize our personal call to holiness. God desires us each to sanctify our lives, to become the best version of ourselves, and to one day join him in heaven.

As described in the *Catechism of the Catholic Church*, we each have an individual call to holiness. We "have the power to uproot the rule of sin within [our lives] and in the world, by [our] self-denial and holiness of life" (943). Changing the world begins with each of us maturing into more Christ-like individuals. By looking inward, we will become better equipped to venture outward.

Saint Paul wrote in his letter to the Ephesians, "I ... urge you to live in a manner worthy of the call you have received, with all humility and gentleness, with patience, bearing with one another through love, striving to preserve the unity of the spirit through the bond of peace" (Eph 4:1–3).

He urges us to be completely humble, kind, and patient, and to act with love. These specific virtues are instrumental to our lives as children of God, and they guide us in daily life toward sanctification, our ultimate calling. As we grow toward holiness and become more like Jesus, we are better equipped to hear and answer the individual call to protect the sanctity of life.

In our calling not only as Christians, but also warriors for the sanctity of life, we should make every effort to keep the unity of the Spirit through the bond of peace.

St. Teresa of Calcutta said, "Abortion has become the greatest destroyer of peace, because it destroys two lives, the life of the child and the conscience of the mother." Mother Teresa was right. Abortion has two victims, and often more than two. Mothers, fathers, grandparents, siblings, and society as a whole are devastated by the loss of life. It is our calling to fight not only for the lives of the unborn children, but also their mothers and fathers, and all others who suffer greatly from this tragedy.

We are called to be ambassadors, to show a better way, using our own lives as examples. As ambassadors, we are called to go into the world with peace and love; to spread the truth to those who have not heard. For this calling, we have been equipped with spiritual graces and gifts. For "as each one has received a gift, use it to serve one another as good stewards of God's varied grace" (1 Pt 4:10).

Some of us will lead pregnancy resource centers. Others will pray in front of abortion clinics. Others will help to write laws and fight the culture of death in a courthouse. Still others will write books or create media content to share the truth and save lives. More will pray without ceasing. Some will teach the truth about abortion, and others will study the science of life, equipping us all with pertinent facts. Some will devote themselves to the healing of those who are ravaged by abortion. All must sow peace and spread love to the broken world. Such a powerful mission can only be accomplished by continuously seeking sanctification in one's own heart and soul.

Even while we strive for sanctification, we are challenged in our ministry. We often see heartbreaking sadness. We confront evil in person, online, and in our own thoughts and words. We are shields for those who have lost their courage, the voices of those who have none, and the swords for those who cannot fight their own battles.

But in the sadness, there are victories. We embrace the mother who turns away on the day of her appointment at an abortion clinic. We rejoice at the abortion clinics that close forever. We lift up our prayers in thanksgiving when an abortion doctor puts down his tools of death and shows remorse. Our responsibility lies in the reality that how we approach each situation has the potential to save or lose a life.

We have as our legacy a beautiful Catholic tradition of many saints who went before us and taught us about life, love, and sacrifice. Pope St. John Paul II spoke with passion, saying, "Never tire of firmly speaking out in defense of life from its conception and do not be deterred from the commitment to defend the dignity of every human person with courageous determination. Christ is with you: be not afraid!"

This is our calling, no matter our vocation: to sacrifice much so that others may have life. To face the angry, the broken, the lost, and offer them life and love. To speak truth with gentleness and humility so that even those far astray will hear and listen. To share peace instead of discord. To love deeply and protect the fallen, the weak, the helpless.

Working in cooperation with God toward the fulfillment of his will — the end of abortion — we can rest easy knowing that God has beautiful plans for us. "For I know well the plans I have in mind for you," declares the Lord, "plans for your welfare and not for woe, so as to give you a future of hope" (Jer 29:11).

In answering the call to holiness, we become more able to act like the saints who defended the unborn. Equipped with Christ's love, a plethora of gifts and graces, and a desire to answer the call to this ministry, we will be able to love above all else.

REFLECTION

Why is it important to seek holiness or sanctification before and during our pro-life work?

_____

_____

_____

What are you currently doing, or what can you begin doing, to sanctify your own life? How will you look inward so that you are better equipped to venture outward?

_____

_____

_____

_____

_____

_____

_____

Saint Paul's Letter to the Romans describes some of the different gifts we may receive from God. Read the Bible passage below and think about your own gifts that God has given you. What are these gifts? How have you used and developed these gifts?

> Since we have gifts that differ according to the grace given to us, let us exercise them: if prophecy, in proportion to the faith; if ministry, in ministering; if one is a teacher, in teaching; if one exhorts, in exhortation; if one contributes, in generosity; if one is over others, with diligence; if one does acts of mercy, with cheerfulness. (Romans 12:6–8)

_____

_____

_____

_____

_____

_____

_____

_____

Pope St. John Paul II said, "Christ is with you! Be not afraid!" Read the following Bible passage. What do the Scripture and John Paul II's quote have in common? What does this mean for your call to the pro-life ministry?

> For God did not give us a spirit of cowardice but rather of power and love and self-control. (2 Timothy 1:7)

_____

_____

_____

_____

_____

_____

_____

_____

Read the following passages from the Bible. How do they guide you as you use your gifts to aid the calling for pro-life ministry?

Do not neglect to do good and to share what you have; God is pleased by sacrifices of that kind. (Hebrews 13:16)

As each one has received a gift, use it to serve one another as good stewards of God's varied grace. Whoever preaches, let it be with the words of God; whoever serves, let it be with the strength that God supplies, so that in all things God may be glorified through Jesus Christ, to whom belong glory and dominion forever and ever. Amen. (1 Peter 4:10–11)

_____

_____

_____

_____

_____

_____

_____

_____

THREE

How Does Satan Sabotage Our Efforts?

Remember that the Devil doesn't sleep,
but seeks our ruin in a thousand ways.
— St. Angela Merici

Everyone who is involved in pro-life work stands on a firm foundation of truth, fighting together for innocent and vulnerable lives. How, then, is it possible that our ministry often seems to falter? Why do women continue to choose abortion? Why do we become angry with each other, fight over how to reach women, or scoff at the efforts of our brothers and sisters?

Where have we gone wrong? What pieces are we missing?
The simple answer is: evil.

Satan lives in sin, and he loves sin.

The Devil is preoccupied with keeping us active in sin.

The Devil gets a foothold in our souls through our sins. He will do anything in his power to keep the sin alive. He owns the sin and thus the soul that is overshadowed by it, so he fights desperately to keep his foothold, to protect his claim. He whispers lies and cultivates dissension, anger, insults, and depression. He uses elements of truth to increase the power of his deceptions, all the while building a wall between God's grace and forgiveness and the sinner who is trapped within the sin. All this Satan does in an effort to safeguard his claim on our souls, and when he is successful, the sin becomes all-consuming.

How, then, are we supposed to fight back?

We know that Satan will do anything he can to maintain his foothold in a soul. The moment we take a stand for what is right and stop enabling the sin within us or around us, Satan will become enraged. He will try anything to make us yield and quit. He will use people, giving them hateful, vile words to hurl at us. He will whisper uncertainties, trying to kill our hope. He will bring to our memory our past transgressions and lay them before us in judgment. He may attack us financially, or even legally in the justice system. He may destroy our reputations, friendships, or families. There is no limit to his cruelty, or to his tactics as he fights desperately to keep the souls he has claimed. This is the basis of spiritual warfare.

This is the lifelong struggle we Christians must all endure with fortitude and virtue. No matter how dire the attacks, we must never cooperate with Satan's cruelty, deceptions, and efforts to keep us from Christ. We must learn to recognize the truth with prudence when Satan lies to us, and to recognize the seeds of anger, jealousy, and envy when Satan plants them. We must cultivate compassion, love, and understanding; we must seek a patient heart and guard our tongues against slander, gossip, deceit, and venomous words.

Satan loves abortion. He loves to kill innocent life. Jesus calls Satan "a murderer from the beginning" (Jn 8:44). Satan strives to lay claim to every soul that has committed an abortion or acted to contribute to an abortion. Only through the grace of Our Lord Jesus Christ, who died and rose again, can Satan's wiles be vanquished. The moment they begin to turn away from their pain and sin and seek the grace God offers, Satan will immediately fight back. He wants to keep them for himself.

Through his lies and manipulation, Satan tells people hurt by abortion that they are now "free." He tells them they did no harm, that they aren't responsible for the sins they committed. He tells them abortion helps people to live their best lives. He lies to them in the shadows of their minds. He lies to abortion supporters in politics, on television, and in schools. He lies to them in the quiet of their own homes, in their memories, and in their prayers. He rejoices when these people pretend the abortions didn't happen, or that abortions don't hurt women, fathers, and extended family members. He leads generations of people to believe that abortions are safe, legal, and rare, and rejoices when society believes the lie. He delights when people lock up the secret of their abortions and hide the key, because as long as the sin of abortion is hidden, it belongs to him, and he owns it in its entirety.

In this spiritual enslavement, the soul begins to wither. Many women who have experienced abortion suffer deep spiritual, emotional, and psychological pain. Depression, post-traumatic stress disorder, eating disorders, and broken relationships are common. Others, often those who deny that they experienced any negative side effects, become enraged at the pro-life community who seek to limit their access to abortion or judge them as having committed a sin. Their anger flies toward God's people in heated arguments, screaming protests, or vengeful words. Still others hold so tightly and so deeply to the secret that they continue to live life as if nothing ever happened. Many are oblivious to the state of their souls, to their captivity, as Satan sits back and waits for them to die without a fight, leading them straight to a spiritual slaughter. Others are so broken and lost that they see no hope, no grace powerful enough to cover their wounds.

These are the very captives Jesus came to set free. For these captives, Christ was crucified, bled, and died. For these captives, Christ endured the passion and rose again. These are the sheep Christ came to find.

REFLECTION

What does the Bible say about enslavement and sin? According to the verses below, how does one become a slave to sin?

We know that our old self was crucified with him, so that our sinful body might be done away with, that we might no longer be in slavery to sin. (Romans 6:6)

Jesus answered them, "Amen, amen, I say to you, everyone who commits sin is a slave of sin." (John 8:34)

For freedom Christ set us free; so stand firm and do not submit again to the yoke of slavery. (Galatians 5:1)

They promise them freedom, though they themselves are slaves of corruption, for a person is a slave of whatever overcomes him. (2 Peter 2:19)

For we ourselves were once foolish, disobedient, deluded, slaves to various desires and pleasures, living in malice and envy, hateful ourselves and hating one another. (Titus 3:3)

_____

_____

_____

_____

_____

_____

_____

According to the verses below, what can I do to help bring about God's will for all people to be set free from sin?

> This is my commandment: love one another as I love you. (John 15:12)

> The Spirit of the Lord is upon me,
>   because he has anointed me
>   to bring glad tidings to the poor.
> He has sent me to proclaim liberty to the captives
>   and recovery of sight for the blind,
>   to let the oppressed go free. (Luke 4:18)

> The spirit of the Lord God is upon me,
>   because the Lord has anointed me;
> He has sent me to bring good news to the afflicted,
>   to bind up the brokenhearted,

To proclaim liberty to the captives,
release to the prisoners. (Isaiah 61:1)

For God is not unjust so as to overlook your work and the love you have demonstrated for his name by having served and continuing to serve the holy ones. (Hebrews 6:10)

Do nothing out of selfishness or out of vainglory; rather, humbly regard others as more important than yourselves, each looking out not for his own interests, but [also] everyone for those of others. (Philippians 2:3–4)

In what areas of your life or ministry have you experienced spiritual warfare, or attacks from Satan? How has the enemy attacked your faith, ministry, or relationships? Were you able to trust and rely on God to win these battles for you?

Do you have a persistent sin that continues to entrap you? What have you done in an attempt to break free from this sin?

What weapons, both spiritual and physical, do we have at our disposal to fight Satan? Have you used these weapons? How can you use these weapons in the future?

_____

_____

_____

_____

_____

_____

FOUR

God and the Church Desire Life for All

The Lord has loved me so much: We must love everyone. We must be compassionate!
— St. Josephine Bakhita

The Lord desires that every one of his creations will live in the fullness of truth and be with him for eternity. He does not wish eternal death for anyone. His love is so abounding, his mercy so great, that he sent his only Son to die in our place (see Jn 3:16).

Through Christ's passion, Satan has already been defeated,

and victory declared over death. For all those who accept the gift of God, he gives eternal life (see Rom 6:23).

God also gave humanity another gift: free will. It is this freedom to choose our own actions that gives us the ability to freely seek out our Creator of our own accord. For "God in the beginning created human beings and made them subject to their own free choice" (Sir 15:14).

Christ desires that all people will come to know the fullness of the truth and accept Christ's gift of eternal life. He wants to free captives from their sin. The *Catechism* says:

> God predestines no one to go to hell; for this, a willful turning away from God (a mortal sin) is necessary, and persistence in it until the end. In the Eucharistic liturgy and in the daily prayers of her faithful, the Church implores the mercy of God, who does not want "any to perish, but all to come to repentance":

> > [Father,] graciously accept this oblation of our service,
> > that of your whole family, ...
> > order our days in your peace,
> > and command that we be delivered from eternal damnation,
> > and counted among the flock of those you have chosen. (1037)

In every Mass, we the faithful stand together and pray that all people will be counted among the chosen. We must genuinely understand and believe this truth. God created every single human being perfectly and with dignity. He loves each one of them, even when they use their free will to turn away from him.

We must be vigilant in this reality. We cannot say that we

desire every person to be among the chosen and live for eternity with Christ only to turn around and snap at our brothers and sisters, or condemn those who are deeply enslaved to sin.

As pro-life advocates, we must understand that every human being is loved by God. Every woman who has had an abortion is loved by God. Every abortion doctor is loved by God. Every volunteer at an abortion facility who escorts women inside the clinic, making a human shield so that the pregnant woman cannot hear the help being offered, is loved by God. Every politician who votes for death-affirming laws is loved by God. Every pro-life advocate who is not acting with love toward others is loved by God.

Imagine a child, innocent and pure, playing at the foot of Jesus' throne. The child looks happily up at Jesus, face to face, and shares his toys with him. The child is happy to be in the presence of his Father. As the child grows, he begins to sin. With each sin, the child's body turns slightly away from Jesus. Soon, he has to look over his shoulder to be able to see Jesus on the throne, or to speak to him. As the child grows into a man, the sin has become so entrenched, he can no longer see Jesus at all. His back faces Christ, and he looks out into a vast, empty world. He feels that his Lord has abandoned him. But Jesus, never ceasing, never failing, remains with his eyes on the child the entire time. Jesus remains steadfast while the child sins, while he grows into a man, and while he stands, facing the darkness, turned away. Jesus does not leave him, or even taken his eyes off him. He simply waits for the man to turn around and look at him.

It is our job first to turn squarely to Christ and root out our own sinfulness. Only then, when we are facing Christ, should we take the hand of those who have their backs to Jesus and help them turn around. We do this through compassion, truth with love, patience, kindness, peace, and forgiveness. We do this by ministering to those who are enslaved by abortion. We do this by allowing the Holy Spirit to work in us and guide our every move. We do this with love.

As pro-life advocates, we diligently work toward the eradication of abortion. We want to make abortion unthinkable. It is through our faith, our hope, our love, our actions, our deeds, our words, and our thoughts that we will be able to cooperate with the Holy Spirit and achieve the goal of eradicating abortion.

REFLECTION

What does the Bible say about those who are separated from God?

No, the hand of the LORD is not too short to save,
   nor his ear too dull to hear.
Rather, it is your crimes
   that separate you from your God,
It is your sins that make him hide his face
   so that he does not hear you. (Isaiah 59:1–2)

It was fitting that we should have such a high priest: holy, innocent, undefiled, separated from sinners, higher than the heavens. (Hebrews 7:26)

Consider how God loves all human beings. How do you feel about God's love for abortion doctors or women who have had abortions? Write down the feelings that come up as you think about those who have destroyed or continue to destroy unborn children.

_____

_____

_____

_____

_____

_____

_____

Imagine an abortion doctor who has not repented. He has completed thousands of abortions on children at all stages of development. Now, imagine that doctor as an infant, the moment he was born. Imagine his first breath, and his mother's tears of joy as she held him for the first time. Imagine his tiny fingers and toes, his cooing voice. When you think of him *this* way, are you able to cultivate compassion for him? How does this thought exercise help you see abortionists in a different light?

_____

_____

_____

_____

_____

_____

_____

_____

Is there anything keeping you from desiring life for all human beings, including those who participate in abortion?

_____

_____

_____

_____

_____

_____

_____

_____

FIVE

Compassion in All Things

Even while living in the world, the heart of Mary was so filled with motherly tenderness and compassion for men that no one ever suffered so much for their own pains, as Mary suffered for the pains of her children.
— St. Jerome of Stridon

I once told a woman in an online forum that we should always remain compassionate toward women who have had abortions. In response to my statement on the forum, I received a private online message from a separate, very angry pro-life woman. The angry message said that I was a "fake pro-lifer" because I'd had an abortion a decade ago. She told me that there was no way I had been manipulated or coerced into the decision to take RU486; that I was a big girl, had a college degree, and should have known better. She was so adamant in her anger and judgment toward me that my first impulse was to lash out back at her. But love is patient, and love is kind.

I prayed about her message and thought about how best to respond, because every word is significant and can do evil or good. When it comes to issues of life and death, especially abortion, we must be extremely careful with our words and actions. It was time to show this woman compassion, not anger, and to put into action the advice I had advocated for on the online forum just moments before.

I responded that I am not a "fake" pro-lifer and explained how, since my own abortion, I have advocated for life-affirming laws and court cases, witnessing in Congress and at the state level. I assured her that interacting with compassion is the most effective way to communicate with those debating abortion. I explained that she and I are not enemies but fight for the same truth.

She responded that she had a miscarriage at a young age, but had her baby lived, she would never have aborted her child. She directed her seething anger right at me, and at every woman who had done what I had done. In this moment, I understood. I understood her pain and agony. I was overcome with compassion for her loss.

I asked her if her anger was coming from a place of pain, because I had thrown away the one thing she longed to have. Her child was taken unfairly, and I had tossed away my own. In this moment of empathy and compassion, her anger melted away. She said, "It pains me to say, you may be right."

In Luke, chapter 13, Jesus tells the story of the barren fig tree. The beauty of parables is that they can teach us many things, and the Holy Spirit can lead us to deeper understanding each time we read them. The parable goes:

> There once was a person who had a fig tree planted in his orchard, and when he came in search of fruit on it but found none, he said to the gardener, "For three years now I have come in search of fruit on this fig tree but have found none. [So] cut it down. Why should it exhaust the soil?" He said to him in reply, "Sir, leave it for this year also, and I shall cultivate the ground around it and fertilize it; it may bear fruit in the future. If not you can cut it down." (Luke 13:6–9)

We traditionally interpret this parable as God the Father checking on us throughout our lives to see if we are bearing good fruit, and if not, we are cut down at the end. But the wonderful thing about parables is that they can mean many different things to different people, depending on how the Holy Spirit leads us to read them.

Imagine the fig tree represents a post-abortive mother. She has lost her child and is barren. The gardener begs the owner of the tree to not cut it down yet, but rather to wait and to fertilize and care for the tree. He pleads and says the tree may still bear fruit in the future — if you do not cut it down.

If you do not cut it down.

Don't cut post-abortive women down. Don't hurl judgment and anger and hate at them. Don't point your finger at them and tell them they are horrible, sinful beings. Guard your heart against hateful thoughts and feelings toward these women, as toward all God's children.

Care for them. Like the gardener fertilizing the tree, give them compassion, empathy, and love. Show them the truth, which they may already recognize. Share the healing power of

God's love and grace. Slowly, watch them heal, grow, and bear good fruit.

It is perhaps the voice of the post-abortive woman that weighs the heaviest, whose testimony is often most powerful in our fight to protect the unborn. Would you rather turn her away? Cut her down? Or would you rather help her grow into a powerful, passionate, and compassionate advocate for life? She has lived through the horror of abortion and carries within her body and soul an experience many pro-life advocates can never truly understand.

You don't cause a garden to bear fruit by destroying the trees. Neither does the garden bear fruit when we shrug our shoulders and let a barren tree wither and die on its own. No, we work in the garden, and we cultivate, fertilize, and try hard to salvage what is dying.

Compassion is not only for mothers who have aborted their children. It is also necessary to reach out to fellow pro-lifers who seethe with anger, those who lash out from places of pain or sorrow. They, too, need a gardener to help them bear good fruit, to prune away their thorns. A compassionate, loving, understanding gardener.

Do not cut down the tree. Cultivate the ground around it and fertilize it; it may bear fruit in the future.

REFLECTION
What would it mean to be a gardener and cultivate the earth in the pro-life ministry?

_____

_____

_____

_____

Does reading the parable of the barren fig tree change your viewpoint about post-abortive women? If so, how?

_____

_____

_____

_____

_____

_____

Have you encountered angry pro-life advocates like the woman in this chapter? Or have you yourself been angry at post-abortive women in your ministry? What are some of the root causes for this anger? Brainstorm as many as you can (examples: loss of a child, a past, forced abortion, abandonment, abuse, etc.). Circle the causes that apply to you.

_____

_____

_____

_____

_____

_____

_____

_____

Read the parable of the weeds among the wheat found in the Gospel of Matthew. What can this parable teach us in regard to our pro-life ministry, specifically verse 29?

> He proposed another parable to them. "The kingdom of heaven may be likened to a man who sowed good seed in his field. While everyone was asleep his enemy came and sowed weeds all through the wheat, and then went off. When the crop grew and bore fruit, the weeds appeared as well. The slaves of the householder came to him and said, 'Master, did you not sow good seed in your field? Where have the weeds come from?' He answered, 'An enemy has done this.' His slaves said to him, 'Do you want us to go and pull them up?' He replied, 'No, if you pull up the weeds you might uproot the wheat along with them. Let them grow together until harvest; then at harvest time I will say to the harvesters, "First collect the weeds and tie them in bundles for burning; but gather the wheat into my barn."'" (13:24–30)

SIX

On Our Thoughts

All the darkness in the world cannot
extinguish the light of a single candle.
— St. Francis of Assisi

In Mark, chapter 8, Simon Peter is the first to recognize Jesus as the Messiah. Jesus asks, "Who do people say that I am?" The disciples answer with rumors: Elijah, a prophet, John the Baptist. Jesus then asks them directly, "Who do you say that I am?" And Simon Peter answers, "You are the Messiah" (see vv. 27–29).

It took great wisdom and prudence for Peter to see and understand this truth. The rumors about Jesus were many, and the Bible even points out that the disciples' hearts were hardened to the truth about Jesus, despite witnessing his miracle of multiplying the loaves and fishes, and his miracle of walking on water (see Mk 6:52). Jesus then openly began to teach his disciples about his passion and what was to come. Yet even with the recognition of Jesus as Messiah, Peter was unable to understand Jesus when he taught about what he must suffer. In chapter 8, Mark writes that "Peter took [Jesus] aside and began to rebuke him. At this he turned around and, looking at his disciples, rebuked Peter and said, 'Get behind me, Satan. You are thinking not as God does, but as human beings do'" (8:32–33).

Peter fell victim to his human thoughts. Satan was able to enter Peter's mind with doubt and contradiction simply because Peter could not reconcile his preconceived notions of what the Messiah would be and who Jesus really was. Doubt, skepticism, uncertainty, hesitation.

Jesus immediately recognizes Satan and his work in Peter and tells him to get away. He then specifically targets Peter's thoughts, for Peter was "thinking not as God does, but as human beings do." This is an important warning for all of us: Guard your thoughts, and do not give in to the influence of Satan in your minds.

The Catholic Church holds that some doubt can spur us toward the discovery of a deeper faith through allowing us to ask questions and ponder uncertainty. This is called involuntary doubt (CCC 2088). But other forms of doubt are dangerous.

Satan loves to create doubt that causes us to voluntarily reject the truth of the Faith. This doubt disregards what God has revealed, and what the Church teaches. Doubting that we have been forgiven, or doubting that God can redeem everyone regardless of their past, are common issues that we may encounter in our ministry. When we doubt in this way, we can be deprived of the theological virtues of faith and hope. To lose faith is contrary to the first commandment.

We will never be able to fully understand the larger picture or the work God is doing while in this life, but as we fight to protect innocent lives and point souls toward the Savior, we must have faith and hope that Christ will work all things together for good (see Rom 8:28). We must have faith and hope in the redeeming graces God pours out for all people, and in God's promise of everlasting life. We must also have faith and hope in the truth that God does not predestine any of his beloved souls to go to hell. Through faith and hope, we must believe and find comfort in the truth that Jesus has already defeated death, Satan, and all the injustices plaguing the whole world.

It is Satan who plants doubt, skepticism, despair, failure, fear, and any other thought that would deter us from doing God's work in this culture of death. If Peter could stand face to face with Jesus Christ, witness his miracles abounding, and still doubt God's plan, then we can understand how women are much more easily deceived by our culture's lies about abortion.

Our culture has taught women that they are not strong enough to be mothers and also fulfill their dreams. They are made to believe that once they have a child, they will never finish college, have the career they desire, or meet the man of their dreams. They are made to feel incapable, as if a pregnancy and a child will destroy their life, their hope, and their future. They are told that their pregnancy will meet harsh judgment from the world and their families if they get pregnant in any but what society deems the "perfect" circumstances. In general, it's safer if they get rid of it.

When women enter abortion facilities, they are bombarded by lies wrapped up in tidy packages of false sympathy and understanding. They hand over their money and walk out as slaves to the sin of abortion they have committed.

There is only one author of these lies that cause such damaging doubt and fears. There is only one author of these thoughts that cripple women and steal their hope, their courage, and their children.

The Bible tells us to "Be sober and vigilant. You opponent the devil prowls around like a roaring lion looking for [someone] to devour" (1 Pt 5:8). As warriors for life and love, we must always guard our thoughts. We must always pray for wisdom and a sound mind, never allowing Satan to plant within us the evils of doubt, skepticism, despair, or fear.

We must also stand as guardians and protectors of those who are under the influence of the Devil, for their hope has been diminished. Proverbs 24:11 says, "Rescue those who were being dragged off to death, / those tottering, those near death." And 1 Peter 4:8 says, "Above all, let your love for one another be intense, because love covers over a multitude of sins."

REFLECTION

If the author of lies were standing in front of you, would you be able to identify him? What would he look like? What would he say about abortion? Read the Scripture passages below, which offer guidance for recognizing and rejecting the voice of the evil one.

You belong to your father the devil and you willingly carry out your father's desires. He was a murderer from the beginning and does not stand in truth, because there is no truth in him. When he tells a lie, he speaks in character, because he is a liar and the father of lies. (John 8:44)

And no wonder, for even Satan masquerades as an angel of light. (2 Corinthians 11:14)

_____

_____

_____

_____

_____

_____

_____

What do the following verses tell us about guarding our thoughts?

Have no anxiety at all, but in everything, by prayer and petition, with thanksgiving, make your requests known to God. Then the peace of God that surpasses all understanding will guard your hearts and minds in Christ Jesus. (Philippians 4:6–7)

Do not conform yourselves to this age, but be transformed by the renewal of your mind, that you may discern what is the will of God, what is good and pleasing and perfect. (Romans 12:2)

_____

_____

_____

_____

_____

_____

_____

How can you protect your own thoughts from the influence of the Devil?

_____

_____

_____

_____

_____

_____

_____

How can you be a guardian for others against the lies of the Devil?

_____

_____

_____

_____

_____

_____

Read Philippians 4:8. How can you cultivate faith, hope, and love in your mind?

> Finally, brothers, whatever is true, whatever is honorable, whatever is just, whatever is pure, whatever is lovely, whatever is gracious, if there is any excellence and if there is anything worthy of praise, think about these things. (Philippians 4:8)

SEVEN

On Our Words

If this is the way you treat your friends,
no wonder you have so few!
— St. Teresa of Ávila

When my second child was just a baby, I visited a faithful Catholic friend for tea. I was unmarried at the time, with two living children from different fathers. My friend knew the truth about my situation: I was a post-abortive single mother, but a devoted, loving mother who was growing in zeal for Christ every day. She loved me, and she loved my children deeply. As we sat and caught up on life, we watched my three-year-old running around the house chasing the dog as my baby slept.

My friend shared with me that her son was expecting a child out of wedlock. She was upset about his situation and said without thinking, "The last thing we need is more fatherless kids running around."

I was immediately hurt by her words. I sat very still and looked directly into her eyes. I said nothing. I waited and let the children and my situation be a mirror in which she could see the truth of her words. Several seconds ticked by, and we locked eyes. Suddenly, her face changed, and a look of pain came over her.

"Oh no! That's not what I meant!"

"I know," I responded. "But that is what you said."

This woman who deeply loved my children, who cared for them when I had to work, who bought them gifts at Christmas and on their birthdays, had cursed them without thinking about the magnitude or the weight of her words. Without thinking, she placed them in a category of lower-class, less important people, people that society would be better off without. Those who were born out of wedlock. The fatherless. As if their worth and dignity as human beings depended on the circumstances of their birth.

Words are powerful.

In the Letter of James, chapter 3, we read about the power of the tongue. "If anyone does not fall short in speech, he is a perfect man, able to bridle his whole body also" (Jas 3:2). We know that no one but Jesus Christ is perfect. We all fall short in our speech. James also writes that the tongue is like a small fire that can set a huge forest ablaze. He warns, "[The tongue] exists among our members as a world of malice, defiling the whole body and setting the entire course of our lives on fire" (3:6).

We cannot master the control of our tongue alone. The tongue is restless and evil (see Jas 3:8). Only through the grace of God can we bridle the tongue. We need to pray fervently for help in taming our speech.

One simple way to do so is to pray Psalm 141, verse 3: "Set a guard, LORD, before my mouth, / keep watch over the door of my lips."

Once you have prayed, have faith that the Lord will in fact set a guard over your mouth. "Therefore I tell you, all that you ask for in prayer, believe that you will receive it and it shall be yours" (Mk 11:24).

Praying for guidance probably will not physically keep us from using the tongue for evil, but it will allow the grace of God to speak directly to our consciences. As we practice bridling and taming the tongue, the Spirit will become louder and clearer within us, helping us to curb the words that might harm others.

Our words are often the only tool we have for reaching out to women considering abortion, or those hurt by abortion. We often have just one chance to interact with someone. One small chance to show them the love of Christ through our own words.

This doesn't mean that we need to share everything there is to know about Jesus in one happenstance meeting. It doesn't mean we need to point out in the first minute that abortion is murder, and the wages of sin is death. It means that when God puts us in the place he has directed us to go, and we are in a position to use our words, we have a responsibility to use them as Christ would — in truth, love, compassion, mercy, and peace.

When it comes to our words, less is often more. Be quick to listen and slow to speak (see Jas 1:19). Cultivate compassion for those who do not yet know the fullness of the truth.

When we have the opportunity to speak with a woman considering abortion, it is imperative that we speak life and hope to her. "Death and life are in the power of the tongue.; / those who choose one shall eat its fruit" (Prv 18:21). What does it mean to speak life? Encourage her and empower her. Help her conquer fear with love and faith. Offer help and service. Be sincere in your love for her and her unborn child. Speak the truth about the reality of abortion if it is appropriate, using your own or another's experiences. Many in our pro-life community are aflame with the love of Christ and want to share the Gospel at all times. For some, Christ is always on their lips, and not to share the Gospel would be unnatural. Yet, sharing the truth of Christ must be done with prudence, when the time is right, and when the Holy Spirit advises us to do so.

Pray for the gifts of prudence and temperance, which are cardinal virtues. Prudence allows us to look at each situation and know what is right and good to do. Temperance helps us moderate our desires, as well as the passions we feel while engaged in pro-life work. In short, each situation is different, but we are equipped through the Holy Spirit to respond to each situation with love.

REFLECTION

Write a special prayer asking the Lord to set a guard over your mouth. Ask for the gifts of temperance, prudence, and wisdom in speaking. Commit to praying it as often as you can, daily if possible.

During Mass, right before the Gospel is read, the priest declares the Gospel reading aloud, and the congregation responds by crossing their foreheads, lips, and chests, saying, "Glory to you, O Lord." This is an outward sign for an inward prayer asking the Lord to help us think with God's wisdom, speak with God's truth, and love as Christ does. Do you practice the inward meditation behind this outward sign? If so, write the meditation that you pray during this moment in Mass. If not, you can write your own or use this example:

> Lord, be always in my mind and give me wisdom, be always on my lips and help me speak truth, and be always in my heart so I can love as deeply as you.

Are there any other times when this prayer would be appropriate to use in your daily life?

Imagine yourself praying outside an abortion clinic. A woman leaves the clinic, screams profanities at you, and makes a rude gesture with her hands. She approaches you angrily, and asks: "Do you even care about women? Do you know how scared they are? Do you know how badly these women need these abortion services? All you care about is yourself and your agenda!" You want to tell her how abortion hurts women, but can see that she is angry. Write down three things you could say to this woman, relying on prudence and temperance.

When a woman is experiencing a crisis, her immediate needs include feeling safe and knowing she has support and resources. Would you be able to set aside your desire to discuss Jesus Christ and focus on her immediate, tangible needs? How do you feel when you imagine doing this? What might happen if you discuss Jesus before addressing her other needs?

_____

_____

_____

_____

_____

_____

_____

How have words spoken carelessly affected you? Think about the wound in your heart and mind. Was the pain lasting? Did the person who spoke the words do so intentionally or unintentionally?

_____

_____

_____

_____

_____

_____

_____

_____

Have you ever spoken words that harmed another? Did you speak them intentionally or unintentionally? What did you learn from the experience?

_____

_____

_____

_____

_____

_____

_____

EIGHT

When the Time Comes to Correct or to Be Corrected

You cannot be half a saint. You must
be a whole saint, or no saint at all.
— St. Thérèse of Lisieux

Our pro-life community is vast and full of people from all walks of life. God has willed it to be so, so that he can work in all of us for different purposes. Where one of us can go successfully, others cannot. Some people have yet to experience things that others have experienced many times. We are kaleidoscopes of many varied talents, actions, life experiences, and ideas.

Because there are so many who identify as pro-life, we are bound to encounter those within our ministry who are in error, either in thoughts, words, or actions. Even in the smallest communities, because we are all flawed people, there will inevitably be a time when one of us acts or speaks in error. These times are opportunities to minister to each other and help us all grow as children of God.

Very early in my ministry, I shared a woman's abortion story, not realizing that she had told me the story in confidence. I didn't realize that her story was not public. I didn't intend to hurt her or cause her harm. However, I was quickly contacted by a more experienced pro-life advocate who explained to me that to share her story was out of line. She told me that I needed to only speak from my own experience, and maintain at all times the confidentiality of those who open up to me.

It was a difficult conversation. At first, I felt deeply saddened that I had made a mistake and hurt another woman. Then I felt ashamed and full of guilt. But the way I was corrected allowed me to grow. I was corrected quietly, respectfully, and my mistake was explained to me in a way that I understood. I was able to seek forgiveness and right the wrong as much as possible, thanks to the brave advocate and her gentleness.

When we are called to correct one another, we must do so with love. Admonishing or correcting one another does not mean cutting each other down. It does not mean we stand in front of a person and confront his or her moral failings with anger, judgment, or self-righteousness. To admonish another means that we see an area where he or she is struggling, and we, out of deep love for that person, are willing to roll up our own sleeves and offer help. Admonishing another does not mean pointing fingers while preaching, lest we fall into the sins of boasting or hypocrisy. As the saying goes, if we point one finger at another, three more will point back at us. We must be ever careful to remove the plank from our own eye so as to clearly see the speck in our brother's (see Mt 7:5).

Hypocrisy is a dangerous thing. Read Matthew 23:1–36. Jesus denounces the scribes and Pharisees for parading around, reveling in their honor, while neglecting the most important things, like mercy. He warns the people to do as the scribes and Pharisees say, not as they do, for they are hypocrites. Keep watch! Pray that we never become hypocrites!

If we bridle our tongues, set guards over our mouths, and allow the Holy Spirit to speak through us with love, we will be able to plant seeds that will grow, sowing the truth without the weeds of discord, and will help each other grow toward holiness.

It takes a lot of courage to approach someone who is in error. Consider this when we are approached by another who points out a fault or error in ourselves. It can be incredibly humbling and difficult to accept correction. No one wants to examine her own mistakes or faults. But it is in these moments that we grow immensely.

For many people, the first reaction to a correction is to defend ourselves, either with explanations, excuses, or even anger. But if we truly wish to walk in the will of God, we need to always stay humble. Simply listen to the correction. There is no need to argue or fight back. Much can be gained and learned from listening. Take the correction to prayer, or to another trusted follower of Christ. Resist the temptation to diminish your own actions or explain things away. When we give ourselves time to listen, and time for our consciences to move in us, we will often come to terms with our error, and can graciously accept correction and act on what God is asking us to do.

REFLECTION

Read the following verses and think about what setting a guard over your mouth truly means for you. Write down stumbling blocks you may have that challenge you when it comes to guarding your mouth.

Set a guard, LORD, before my mouth,
keep watch over the door of my lips. (Psalm 141:3)

Those who guard mouth and tongue
guard themselves from trouble. (Proverbs 21:23)

Those who guard their mouths preserve themselves;
those who open wide their lips bring ruin. (Proverbs 13:3)

_____

_____

_____

_____

_____

_____

_____

How might the following verses help you in a conversation with a woman considering abortion?

No foul language should come out of your mouths, but

only such as is good for needed edification, that it may benefit those who listen. (Ephesians 4:29)

Be reverent in [your] behavior, not slanderers ... teaching what is good. (Titus 2:3)

Know this, my dear brothers: everyone should be quick to hear, slow to speak, slow to wrath. (James 1:19)

Proverbs 18:21 says, "Death and life are in the power of the tongue." What does this mean in your pro-life ministry?

_____

_____

_____

Have you ever been corrected by a member of the pro-life ministry? Have you ever felt the need to correct another person in the ministry? What happened? What was said? What was the outcome? Were the words kind and gentle, or accusatory or inflammatory?

_____

_____

_____

_____

_____

_____

Read Matthew 15:1–20. Jesus introduces the image of the blind leading the blind. How does this relate to our pro-life ministry? What could happen if we allow our ministry to be led by hypocrites, or if we attempt to lead others without addressing our own faults?

_____

_____

_____

_____

_____

_____

_____

_____

In Mathew 23:1–36, how many times does Jesus say, "Woe to you," when addressing the Pharisees? Why do you think Jesus chose to repeat the phrase this many times?

_____

_____

_____

_____

_____

_____

_____

_____

NINE

When Speaking to a Pregnant Woman in Crisis About Adoption

Love your children. In them
you can see baby Jesus.
— St. Gianna Molla

When life and death hang in the balance, the power of our words can be extreme. We as pro-life individuals often have no idea that the words we say, or the way we say them, can steer women straight into abortion facilities.

When speaking with a woman in a crisis or unsupported pregnancy, we must first set a guard on our tongues and pray fervently that our words never cause unplanned or unforeseeable harm or death. As loving Christians, we must never speak with hate. Yet even when we speak with love, there are three categories of comments that almost always bring about more harm than life. These are comments regarding adoption, comments regarding a woman's future, and comments regarding a woman's moral character.

Though they sound encouraging, comments such as, "Adoption is the loving option," or, "So many people are willing to adopt," can be extremely hurtful to a woman in crisis. If "adoption is the loving option," then the woman often concludes that she is unloving if she chooses to parent her child. This reinforces the greater lie that a woman is not capable of parenting a child if she is young, if she hasn't completed school, if she has a commitment to her job, if she is single, and so forth.

While these comments are usually spoken in an effort to help women choose life by offering adoption as an option, Satan will try to lay claim to these words. When a woman is in crisis, she needs to hear that she is capable of being pregnant, strong enough to go through labor, and worthy to be a mother. Words about adoption can actually build a wall between her and her child. She thinks, "I must not be enough for my baby. I do love my baby, but they are saying adoption is the loving thing to do. I must not be able to have this baby, because I could never give up my child. I am just not strong enough to do that."

Satan has often managed to twist this message by making women think that it is more loving to abort their children than to put both themselves and their children through the pain of separation through adoption.

Any comment that contributes to this thought process, such as "Have you considered adoption?," or "You should give up your baby for adoption" can be cruel, and could potentially lead a woman to choose abortion.

Adoption is truthfully a very loving and beautiful option. But before we offer it to a woman in crisis, we need to speak life through compassion and love. We need to help the mother by cultivating her courage and calling out the lies of the Devil.

While adoption has its beautiful place and is a self-sacrificial gift to families hoping for children, we need to guard our mouths and ensure that every pregnant woman feels empowered, cared for, loved, strengthened, supported, and nourished in body, mind, and soul in order to have her child and love her child. Every child has the right to remain with his or her mother whenever possible. It is our responsibility to build the scaffolds for mothers so that they can be successful in parenting. We should never presume that they do not want their own children.

Similarly, using words that imply superiority over a woman and her abilities is dangerous and will often aid Satan in his goal of destruction. Comments such as, "Let me take your baby," or, "I would love to adopt your baby," may be spoken with hope and sincerity, but what a woman often hears is, "Here, let someone else take your baby. We can take care of your child better than you." The Devil can also spin these comments to make a woman feel as if someone is trying to steal her child. Her child may begin to feel like a commodity on offer to the highest bidder. We must never assume that she is not capable of mothering simply because of her situation.

Thousands of couples are unable to conceive, and their struggle and pain are real. When someone reaches out and offers to take a baby from a woman considering abortion, it is usually done with a heart of love. Nevertheless, Satan is the master of manipulation. He will whisper to a woman facing a crisis pregnancy that it is her responsibility to provide an infertile couple with her own child. He will place on her a tremendous amount of guilt for her situation, her fertility, and her fear.

It is not the responsibility of a woman in a crisis pregnancy to provide an infertile couple a baby. We must always be on guard and pray that our words never aid Satan's plan or create deeper conflict within another.

There are many beautiful, true stories of life and love when a biological mother placed her child up for adoption instead of choosing abortion. But before a woman can choose adoption, she must first decide to give life to her baby. Her immediate needs must be met. She needs to feel safe, have support, and have access to the resources necessary to carry her child. So how do we broach the subject of adoption with a woman experiencing a crisis pregnancy? It is important to remember that a woman can choose adoption at any time during her pregnancy, in the hospital when she has the child, and even after birth. There is no need to pressure a woman regarding adoption or to create a false sense of immediacy or urgency. Rather, the topic can be addressed once you have established mutual trust and rapport with the mother, and then only if she remains conflicted about carrying out her role as a parent.

REFLECTION

How can we introduce the subject of adoption without diminishing the strength, courage, and convictions of the biological mother?

Take a look at the following phrases: "Adoption is the loving option," and "Adoption is a loving option." Which word is different? Circle it. How does that single small word change the meaning and message of the phrases?

One of the coercive tactics employed by abortion facilities is immediacy. Clinics compel women to choose abortion by stating they have a time limit for certain procedures according to law or gestational age. This forces a woman to believe she needs to make a big decision very quickly. In this way, abortion clinics coerce women into procedures they may not have chosen if time had not been a factor. In light of this, how can we ensure that when we broach the subject of adoption, we do not engage in similar coercive manipulation?

_____

_____

_____

_____

_____

_____

Some women are afraid to offer their child up for adoption because they are afraid their child will be placed in a bad home or experience abuse in the foster care system. They are afraid that it is unloving to give up their child, and fear the separation after birth. They feel that an abortion is a more humane way to ensure less pain and suffering for both themselves and their baby. Reflect on this point of view. How might you broach this subject with a woman who does not want to parent, but is afraid to choose adoption?

_____

_____

_____

_____

_____

_____

_____

TEN

Regarding a
Woman's Future

*I am not capable of doing big things, but
I want to do everything, even the smallest
things, for the greater glory of God.*
— St. Dominic Savio

The painful reality when it comes to comments regarding a woman's future is that they directly play into Satan's power. You have heard them. They range from, "What will you do about school?" to, "Your future is over!" All such comments are lies. They tell a woman that she is incapable of any future that is bright and beautiful. They tell her that the baby she has conceived is going to destroy her future.

The culture of death champions these lies. In schools, doctors' offices, and workplaces, an entire generation of women has been conditioned to believe these lies as cold hard facts. Many men and women alike truly believe that the most compassionate response to a crisis pregnancy is to abort the child so the woman can live the life she dreams of and deserves. They often have no idea that by doing this, they are selling the woman short, grossly underestimating her abilities, and profiting from her fear.

The truth is, there is absolutely nothing a woman cannot do if she also has a baby. She can complete school, get a job, have a career, buy a house, and even become an elite athlete. Instead of illustrating the future as a wasteland or a mountain she can never climb, we must always encourage her. We must tell her about available scholarships, share daycare and preschool programs that we know of and love, and encourage her to pursue her dreams because she is capable of achieving them — and more!

If we comment about a pregnant woman's future in any negative way, we are telling her that her future with a baby is bleak, ugly, impossible, and not something to fight for. The way we speak about women in crisis pregnancies, even when we are not speaking directly to these women, has an impact on the culture around us. We contribute to how society sees and treats these women. Our attitudes toward pregnant women out of wedlock, or teen mothers, or other crisis pregnancies, can contribute to the healing of our culture, or contribute to the culture that offers abortion as the only viable option — the culture that lies to women and shames them into abortion, or breeds the fear that pushes them toward that choice.

Pregnancy, birth, and childrearing are not easy. But they are heroic, and often fulfilling in ways we can never anticipate. There is no need to ignore the challenges and difficulties of pregnancy, birth, and parenting, but with support, facing the challenges becomes less frightening.

REFLECTION

Have you ever been on the receiving end of a comment that belittled your future? Did it affect your confidence or change your path? How did you feel when you heard it?

_____

_____

_____

_____

_____

_____

_____

Read the following Scripture verses. How does God's view of the future differ from man's view?

> For I know well the plans I have in mind for you ... plans for your welfare and not for woe, so as to give you a future of hope. (Jeremiah 29:11)

> Blessed be the God and Father of our Lord Jesus Christ, who in his great mercy gave us a new birth to a living hope through the resurrection of Jesus Christ from the dead, to an inheritance that is imperishable, undefiled, and unfading, kept in heaven for you. (1 Peter 1:3–4)

_____

_____

_____

_____

_____

_____

_____

_____

What can you do in your community to help single mothers, young or teen mothers, or families who need extra help? Do you believe that these actions make a difference in the lives of these families? How?

_____

_____

_____

_____

_____

_____

_____

Do you know any single mothers or teen mothers? Think about their lives, and everything they have done and overcome. Have they been successful? Do they inspire you? Have their lives changed for better or worse since becoming mothers?

During one of my pregnancies, I was forced to search for a job while visibly pregnant. I was not offered a job even though I was very well qualified in education and experience. What can we do to mitigate this injustice, and other injustices like this?

ELEVEN

Regarding a Woman's Moral Character

God desires from you the least degree
of purity of conscience more than
all the works you can perform.
— St. John of the Cross

When a woman is facing a crisis pregnancy, any disparagement of her moral character is both unhelpful and damaging. Any comment regarding her sexuality, religious failure, moral failure, or any other failure is akin to slapping her face while she is already wounded and scared. These comments can only divide her from God's love, mercy, and forgiveness.

When facing my unplanned pregnancies, I was told, "Well, you should have kept your legs closed." "You know how this happens, right?" "I thought you were a good Christian." Such remarks tell a woman that she has failed in the deepest parts of her person.

Perhaps the conception of her child happened after a choice that went against God's plan for her. Or maybe she was raped. Or maybe her birth control failed — she was doing everything that society said she should do and was unaware of the fullness of the truth about human sexuality. Regardless of the circumstances, such comments only make those who utter them guilty of rash judgment. They do not in any way help the woman overcome her crisis.

God says that he will work all things for good for those who are called according to his purpose (Rom 8:28). He gives children even to those who do not follow his commandments, and every child is a beautiful blessing. We should never forget that God does not make mistakes, but works to make good come from our mistakes (see Gn 50:20). Do we as pro-life people really care how a baby was conceived? We ought to demonstrate with our words that every child has dignity, no matter whether she was wanted, or how she was conceived. The child is here now, and the mother is in a delicate, scary, and uncertain position. Instead of saddling her with blame, shame, guilt, and fear, we are called to show her God's unconditional love. We are called to encourage her. We are called to remove the log from our own eyes, look straight into hers, and say, "You can do this!"

REFLECTION

Below is a table showing examples of words that do not speak life and how a woman facing a crisis pregnancy may interpret these words, as well as a column of life-giving words that we can use instead.

Words that do not speak life	What a woman hears	Words that speak life
"Have you thought about adoption?" "You should give your baby up for adoption."	You aren't strong enough to be a mom. Someone else can do it better.	"You will be such a good mother!" "Every baby is a blessing!"
"Adoption is the loving option."	You don't love your child unless you give up your child for adoption.	"Motherhood is the best thing in the world!"
"I will adopt your baby!"	I have dibs on your baby!	"Congratulations! What do you need?"
"So-o-o-o many people are waiting to adopt!"	Your baby is a commodity and there are people who want to have it/purchase it/take it.	"You are so strong and capable!"

Words that do not speak life	What a woman hears	Words that speak life
"At least you are fertile. So-and-so has been trying for years, and she can't wait to adopt. You should let her adopt your baby."	It is your responsibility to help waiting families get a baby by giving up your own. If you don't do this, you are hurting those families and being selfish.	"This child is yours. You don't have to give him or her up. You can do this. We will help you."
"I guess you won't be on the varsity team then."	You are incapable.	"I am here for you and will help you in any way that I can."
"How are you going to pay for school?"	There is no way you can do this. You will never do all the things you wanted to do.	"There are scholarships for single moms out there!"

Words that do not speak life	What a woman hears	Words that speak life
"You can't have a career and be a single mom."	It's too hard for you. Your future is ruined.	"You can do anything you put your mind to, and I will help you any way that I can."
"Do you know how *hard* it is to be a single mom out there?"	You can't do hard things.	"I know several very successful single mothers. Would you like me to introduce you to them?"
"Kiss your dreams good-bye."	A baby will destroy your dreams. You can't have dreams if you have a baby.	"There is nothing about this pregnancy or this baby that will ruin your future. Your future is still as bright and as beautiful as it ever was!"

Words that do not speak life	What a woman hears	Words that speak life
"Men don't want to date single moms."	You are a disgusting, immoral, unlovable failure.	"There is someone out there who will love you for the beautiful, giving person you are *and* love your baby, too."
"You will never find a husband now."	No one wants you and no one will ever want you.	"Every baby is a blessing."
"You know how this happens, right?"	This is entirely your fault.	"You are not alone."
"What were you thinking?"	You did this to yourself, and you will pay now.	"You can do this because you are strong, courageous, and capable."
"I taught you better than this!"	You aren't as good as you should be.	"Your future is not defined by others."

Words that do not speak life	What a woman hears	Words that speak life
"You should have kept your legs closed!"	You are immoral and lack all self-control!	"You are already such an amazing mother! Look at how you are already taking care of your baby by taking care of your body!"

How can you use this table in your ministry?

_____

_____

_____

_____

_____

_____

_____

Have you ever heard words that do not speak life spoken by a pro-life advocate? Write them below.

_____

_____

_____

_____

_____

_____

_____

_____

Have you ever spoken words that did not speak life? Did you realize they could be damaging?

_____

_____

_____

_____

_____

_____

_____

Read the story of the Samaritan woman at the well in John 4:1–42. Jesus tells the woman the truth about her own immorality. Does Jesus speak harshly to the woman? Does Jesus condemn the woman? What does Jesus offer her instead? What does the woman do after her encounter with Christ?

TWELVE

Breeding Hatred

*Other sins find their vent in the accomplishment
of evil deeds, whereas pride lies in wait
for good deeds, to destroy them.*
— St. Augustine of Hippo

How many times has the pro-life community shouted the phrase, "Abortion is murder!" Swords drawn, ready to do battle for the unborn, we march against the injustice of murdering innocent babies in their mothers' wombs. Rightfully so.

Abortion is murder.

A battle cry is shouted by soldiers entering battle — or a sports team about to take the field — to create solidarity with

97

each other and to intimidate the enemy or opponent. Used in this manner, it can solidify cohesion between those who work toward the common goal of making abortion unthinkable. It can remind us why we're fighting.

In the pro-life ministry, it is common to hear the battle cry, "Abortion is murder!" But when facing the culture of abortion and death as warriors for Christ, we have to remember who the enemy is. The enemy is Satan — not the mothers who choose abortion, not the doctors who prescribe RU486, not the legislators who enact pro-abortion laws, not the politicians, not the women who escort patients into abortion clinics, or the advocates for abortion holding "My body, my choice" signs.

The enemy is Satan.

Because Satan is always manipulating, captivating, plotting, and deceiving, we must understand how he uses our own battle cry to undermine us. First, he uses it as a way to breed hatred in the hearts of the faithful. Second, he uses the repetition and ubiquity of its harshness to desensitize us to its message. Third, he uses it to breed fear and destroy hope in the hearts of those who would return to Christ.

To see examples of the misuse of this battle cry, scroll through a post on a pro-life Facebook group, and you will see dozens of comments, usually in all capital letters with many exclamation points, declaring that abortion is murder. Many times, there is no actual content other than the battle cry.

Words are powerful. They have the ability to conjure strong emotions. When someone looks us in the eyes and says, "I love you, and you are so precious to me," our hearts fill with love and kindness. When someone shouts threats at us, we feel fear, anxiety, or anger in response. Satan is the master of manipulation and deceit. When we carelessly say, "Abortion is murder," without the protection of the Holy Spirit, without first cultivating the virtues of faith, hope, love, prudence, justice, temperance, and fortitude,

Satan swoops into our souls. He begins to cultivate anger and hatred toward those who believe in abortion as a right. He cultivates the anger and hatred until they become more powerful in the heart than love, prudence, justice, temperance, and all the other virtues we need to fight this fight. He revels in the hatred and how it overpowers the faithful. Before long, our battle cry is no longer a stand for justice and cohesion; it becomes a shout of condemnation and judgment, of which Satan is the author.

Anger in and of itself is simply a human passion. It can even be beneficial as a biological reaction to stimuli or danger. However, it becomes a problem when it overcomes our sensibilities. When we act on the anger we feel or allow it to grow into hatred, we often sin. We must never allow anger to become hatred.

What is hatred? The *Catechism of the Catholic Church* says: "Deliberate *hatred* is contrary to charity. Hatred of the neighbor is a sin when one deliberately wishes him evil. Hatred of the neighbor is a grave sin when one deliberately desires him grave harm" (2303). Hatred is wishing bad things would happen to someone and seeing only the unlovable or unlovely aspects of a person.

We are all familiar with the words, "You shall love your neighbor as yourself," found in Galatians 5:14. But how many times have we read only that verse and not the verses around it? Verse 15 says, "But if you go on biting and devouring one another, beware that you are not consumed by one another."

Saint Paul is very clear in his Letter to the Galatians:

Now the works of the flesh are obvious: immorality, impurity, licentiousness, idolatry, sorcery, hatreds, rivalry, jealousy, outbursts of fury, acts of selfishness, dissensions, factions, occasions of envy, drinking bouts, orgies, and the like. I warn you, as I warned you before, that those

who do such things will not inherit the kingdom of
God. In contrast, the fruit of the Spirit is love, joy, peace,
patience, kindness, generosity, faithfulness, gentleness,
self-control. Against such there is no law. Now those who
belong to Christ [Jesus] have crucified their flesh with its
passions and desires. If we live in the Spirit, let us also
follow the Spirit. Let us not be conceited, provoking one
another, envious of one another. (5:19–26)

It is easy to look at the woman who has had an abortion and see
the obvious works of the flesh that Paul describes: the sexual immorality, the impurity, the killing of her child. It is less obvious to
peer into one's own heart and see the works of the flesh there: fits
of rage against the woman, perhaps, or the dissensions between
people within the pro-life ministry that stunt the momentum of
their mission. Factions that bicker over tactics, money, motivations, and beliefs, and even those seeking power or fame, create
discord within our ministry.

Perhaps most common and most dangerous of all is the hatred we often harbor in our hearts for those entrenched in and
enslaved by the sin of abortion. Be wary, because John tells us,
"Everyone who hates his brother is a murderer, and you know
that no murderer has eternal life remaining in him" (1 Jn 3:15).

The Bible equates hatred with murder. God does not look at
our sins and rank us as more or less evil. He does not elevate those
who have not had abortions, praising them for their good judgment. He sees into the heart and finds all the hidden works of the
flesh, and it causes him pain. For each work of the flesh separates
us from him. To hate a woman who has had an abortion or to hate
an abortion doctor makes us murderers in God's eyes.

Satan loves to see our hearts turn to hatred. He loves to see
the conflict that is born of hatred. So how do we reclaim our
battle cry and eradicate the hatred Satan has cultivated?

Proverbs 10:12 says, "Hatred stirs up disputes, / but love covers all offenses." So, then, love is the antidote for hatred. "Love is patient, love is kind. It is not jealous, [love] is not pompous, it is not inflated, it is not rude, it does not seek its own interests, it is not quick-tempered, it does not brood over injury, it does not rejoice over wrongdoing but rejoices with the truth. It bears all things, believes all things, hopes all things, endures all things" (1 Cor 13:4–7).

If we ever use the battle cry, "Abortion is murder," in any way that is not patient or kind, then we stir up conflict and potentially hatred. If we ever use this battle cry to boast, to be proud or self-seeking, we stir up conflict and hatred. If we ever use this battle cry to exhibit anger, we stir up conflict and hatred. If we ever use this battle cry to count a tally of sins and keep a record of another's wrong — you guessed it! We stir up conflict and hatred. If we utter this battle cry in a way that does not protect the innocent or the dignity of another human being, we stir up conflict and hatred.

REFLECTION

Read what the Bible says about anger and hatred below. Above all other things, what is necessary to eradicate anger and hatred?

Whoever says he is in the light, yet hates his brother, is still in the darkness. (1 John 2:9)

If anyone says, "I love God," but hates his brother, he is a liar; for whoever does not love a brother whom he has seen cannot love God whom he has not seen. (1 John 4:20)

Hatred stirs up disputes,
    but love covers all offenses. (Proverbs 10:12)

You have heard that it was said, "You shall love your neighbor and hate your enemy." But I say to you, love your enemies, and pray for those who persecute you. (Matthew 5:43–44)

_____

_____

_____

_____

_____

_____

_____

_____

Read Matthew 22:34–40. Write down the first and second commandments that Jesus tells the Pharisees. Circle the action verbs in both of the commandments you have written down.

_____

_____

_____

_____

_____

_____

Read sections 2302–2306 of the *Catechism of the Catholic Church.* How do hatred and peace relate to one another?

Take a closer look at section 2304 of the *Catechism.* What do "respect for and development of human life" require?

THIRTEEN

Repetition and Desensitization

Earth has no sorrow that heaven cannot heal.
— St. Thomas More

Prime-time television airs grisly, graphic murder scenes, torture scenes, violent sexual scenes, and foul language, as found in shows like *Criminal Minds*. Media has effectively desensitized us to violence. The violence is expected, maybe even desired.

When something is part of our everyday stimuli, part of the background, it becomes like white noise that our brains filter out. For decades, those engaged in the pro-life ministry have used tactics such as shouting, blaming, and finger-pointing. Hearing repeated phrases like, "Abortion is murder," has desensitized society to the truth behind our position. The shock factor of equating what many perceive as a medical procedure to the violent act of murder has all but disappeared.

The less shocked we are at the truth of abortion, the happier Satan becomes. We shout, "Abortion is murder!" but it falls on deaf ears, desensitized ears, ears of those who just do not care. Those who shout it have been written off, labeled, "Those crazy anti-abortion people." We are easily dismissed.

Is there another way to share the gruesome truth about abortion? Is there a way to reach the desensitized ears of those who shrug off the truth? The short answer is, yes! The more we reach out to those who are desensitized in a personal, loving manner, the deeper into their hearts we can reach.

In recent years, pro-life groups have held rallies outside of abortion clinics and on the steps of capitol buildings. Many of them are armed with the Bible, graphic images of aborted children, and signs stating, "Abortion is murder!" Abortion advocates have come out in droves to stand face-to-face with those advocating for life. They carry balloons to block signs, scream into megaphones to drown out the chanting, and are completely deaf to the message the pro-lifers want to share. Does an event such as this do more harm or good? Does it force abortion advocates to dig in their heels? Does it compel them to disregard the message they might listen to if it were presented in a more gentle and loving way?

In contrast, a new trend has begun to gain traction within pro-life ministry. The young are speaking up as the "pro-life generation." Post-abortive men and women are carrying signs and messages that read, "I regret my abortion" and "I regret lost fatherhood." They hold banners that say, "Abortion hurts women," and, "Love them both." This shift away from anger has powerful momentum. It allows the other side the opportunity to see truth without alienating them through anger and finger-pointing, or the perception that they are forced to comply with our whims. The story shifts to a more personal one, where people share the truth calmly and describe how it affects them and their families.

Not all interactions happen at rallies with signs and posters and balloons. Many happen online or in person. There are thousands of examples of individuals attacking the other side online in forums, through comments in posts, and in private messages.

When I finally told the secret of my abortion and began a journey toward healing, I felt compelled to create a video that shared the story of my abortion and my subsequent crisis pregnancies. I used short sentences that could easily be written down on notecards and then held up for a video camera. My plan was just to show these cards and let the video speak for itself, and let the viewer read the story. I wouldn't even need to use my own voice.

I described how alone and neglected I felt, abandoned and pregnant. I described my choice to abort my first child, and how I then chose to give life to two more children. It was transparent, honest, and heartfelt. In part, it read:

> People have told me, "Unless you have been there, and know what it is like ...
> don't PREACH anti-abortion to me!"
> I have been told, "You have no idea what it's like!"
> Christian friends say, "I don't know how anyone could DO THAT to a child!"
> Except ...
> I DO.
> I am a single pregnant mother.
> This is my story ...
> I am a single mother of 3.

I aborted my first child.
I was young. I felt …
Afraid
Guilty
Rejected
Alone.
The father of my second child didn't want me or my
daughter either.
I was …
Abandoned
Rejected
Neglected
And forgotten by him.
I felt …
Unworthy
Cheated
Betrayed
Worthless
Guilty
Useless
Alone.
I am pregnant again.
The FEAR is real.
I wonder what our future holds.
I wonder if I am worthy of LOVE.
I hide behind rejection
Loneliness
Guilt …
People look at my left hand and see no ring.
I feel …
Judged
Anxious
Confused

Depressed.
I made a choice …
Once, I made the WRONG choice.
But
Twice, I made the right one!
I chose LIFE.
You can too!!
Be brave and courageous!
Don't let fear, rejection, abandonment, guilt, loneliness, or anxiety …
Steal your child from you!
People will be angry,
They will react poorly,
People will scoff and say mean things.
Be brave and
Choose your child anyway.
I am #Silentnomore.
I don't feel treasured.
But …
I am promised that I am.
I am special.
Deserving.
LOVED by my babies.
LOVED by God.
And so are you!
"He has sent me to bind up the broken hearted, to proclaim freedom for the captives. To provide for those who mourn. To bestow on them a crown of beauty instead of ashes. They will be called oaks of righteousness, a planting of the LORD for the display of His splendor." Isaiah 61:1–3
I love you!
You are not …

ALONE
Anymore.
<3 Elizabeth

The video streamed its way onto Facebook and into the realm of the public faster and with a louder proverbial shout than I ever anticipated. In a matter of hours, my entire family and network of friends had seen the video. Many of my Facebook friends shared it, and it was then viewed by their friends. Before the day was out, it had been viewed over three hundred times, and before the week was out, it had been shared hundreds of times all over the world and viewed over three hundred thousand times.

The video was viral.

My Facebook page was so full of friend requests and message requests I couldn't possibly keep up with them. I received hundreds of messages a day. Most were positive, but some were heinously evil, judgmental, and mean. It was hard to read the messages that were hurtful and let them go. These were the reactions I had feared, that kept me silent for so long, a slave to this secret.

Among the most difficult comments to read were the messages and statements that were filled with hatred and judgment. Over and over, it pelted me.

"Abortion is murder!"

"Didn't you know that abortion is murder?"

"Wow, I mean, good job on the second and third one, but abortion is murder, and you murdered your child!"

"ABORTION IS MURDER."

They hit me like bullets straight to the heart. The reaction was so strong, I couldn't take it any longer. I removed the video from Facebook and sank back into the silence. It would take several more years before I gained enough courage to speak out publicly again about how abortion hurt me. Several years that could have been used for healing and reaching out to others were wasted in the silence.

Soon, I became desensitized. Every time I saw, "Abortion is murder," or similar words in a post or a message, I rolled my eyes. Those who used that phrase became annoying, insignificant, self-righteous, or even immature in my eyes. I wondered why they couldn't contribute anything helpful to the dialogue. I imagined them pointing fingers at people, seething in anger as they hid behind their computer screens. Then, I began to feel anger toward them and their incessant usage of the words, "Abortion is murder." I began to sympathize with the pro-choice narrative that scoffed at such words.

Our own tactics had become a wedge between the truth and my healing. The truth behind the words was no longer a tool to bring an end to abortion but a weapon to judge, separate, and destroy.

Eventually, I was ready to share my story publicly again, but only after I learned to clothe myself with the whole armor of God and to hold the shield of faith. I have faith that I am redeemed, valuable, loved, and worthy of the Blood of Christ, despite what anyone says to or about me. The bullets that hit me no longer hinder me. I am still desensitized to the words, "Abortion is murder," so today I try to build a bridge to truth and healing by using other words. I try to use my writing and speaking to draw people in with love, instead of pushing them away with hate.

REFLECTION
How can these Bible verses guide us when it comes to using our words in the fight to end abortion?

A mild answer turns back wrath,
  but a harsh word stirs up anger.

The tongue of the wise pours out knowledge,
   but the mouth of fools spews folly.
The eyes of the LORD are in every place,
   keeping watch on the evil and the good.
A soothing tongue is a tree of life,
   but a perverse one breaks the spirit. (Proverbs 15:1–4)

[The fear of the LORD is hatred of evil;]
Pride, arrogance, the evil way,
   and the perverse mouth I hate. (Proverbs 8:13)

Whoever conceals hatred has lying lips,
   and whoever spreads slander is a fool. (Proverbs 10:18)

Remind them to be under the control of magistrates and authorities, to be obedient, to be open to every good enterprise. They are to slander no one, to be peaceable, considerate, exercising all graciousness toward everyone. For we ourselves were once foolish, disobedient, deluded, slaves to various desires and pleasures, living in malice and envy, hateful ourselves and hating one another.
   But when the kindness and generous love
      of God our savior appeared,
   not because of any righteous deeds we had done
      but because of his mercy,
   he saved us through the bath of rebirth
      and renewal by the holy Spirit,
   whom he richly poured out on us
      through Jesus Christ our savior,
   so that we might be justified by his grace
      and become heirs in hope of eternal life.
      (Titus 3:1–7)

Have you ever spoken or written, "Abortion is murder," in a way that did not maintain peace? How can you use the battle cry in a way that makes peace and tells the truth?

Why is it important to not overuse specific arguments or phrases?

There are as many individual people on the pro-choice side of the debate as on the pro-life side. They all have individual reasons for believing the way they do. How does varying our ministry and tactics ensure we don't desensitize people to our message?

FOURTEEN

Spreading Hope

We want to create hope for the person
... we must give hope, always hope.
— St. Teresa of Calcutta

On Christmas Eve 2011, I was twenty-four years old and in the midst of a crisis pregnancy, living thousands of miles away from my parents. I had followed my boyfriend to Texas on the promise that he had been offered a job and a life there for us. Once we arrived, he abandoned me and returned to Oregon, where he quickly became engaged to another woman. Additionally, I was still living with the secret guilt and shame of the abortion I had chosen just eleven months before. I was completely alone. The despair I felt was so heavy and so deep, it threw me into a depression. The stress of my situation ate away at me moment by moment. I called my parents, and with my last ounce of hope, asked them if I could come home to the safety of their house to live and have my child.

They said no.

There are no words to describe the despair and utter abandonment I felt. My world was shattered. I felt that I had no one. I hung up the phone and crumpled into a heap on the floor, sobbing to Jesus, begging him to rescue me.

God, in his great mercy, saw my fear and my despair. He had never left me, no matter how many times I stepped off the path he had made for me. He sent me several people who appeared at just the right moments. These people were loving and gentle. They offered me food, baby clothes, companionship, and love. They invited me to their homes for Christmas and drove with me to the pro-life rally in Dallas, Texas in January, where I marched for the life of the son I had killed the year before. They knew nothing of my abortion, or of my pain, and yet they gave me what I desperately needed. They gave me hope.

For Christians, hope is one of three theological virtues (faith, hope, and love) infused into the souls of the faithful by God (see CCC 1813). Hope gives us the desire to seek happiness in God. Hope sustains us in times of discouragement and abandonment (1818). Hope acts as a beautiful life preserver, keeping the faithful ever longing for and ever waiting for eternal life with God.

Even those who have not been baptized experience hope, for God created man to desire him and to desire happiness. This hope helps them seek out and find God, longing for the closeness and love only he can offer. We, as ambassadors of Christ, must share the hope we have in Christ and offer it to those in despair.

If we interact with others in a way that destroys the hope of those who seek to turn back to Christ and ask for forgiveness, we are gravely wrong. If we in any way destroy the hope of those who have not yet found healing from their pain after abortion, but who long for it, we are also very much in the wrong.

Had the wonderful, compassionate, selfless people who supported me during my time of abandonment said, "Abortion is murder," it very well could have been the straw that broke the camel's back for me. They didn't know that I was struggling over my own abortion, waking in the night with horrible, graphic nightmares. Their witness to me didn't need to justify the truth about abortion. They were the bridge, the example, the love I craved in just the right moment. They did God's work, and I experienced Christ's love and hope through them.

We should all be bridges, reaching out to offer hope to those who need it most. We can be the ones who recognize the pain in the post-abortive mother, and through compassion and forgiveness, cultivate in her the hope of Our Lord Jesus Christ. We can be the ones who speak the truth with love and offer hope to those who are hurting, those enslaved to the sin of abortion, and those in despair. We can reach out to women in crisis pregnancies and offer resources and hope where hope is lost. We can show them a better way of living and the beautiful truth of forgiveness. We must bring hope through love and peace.

Shouting and repeating phrases like, "Abortion is murder," with anger and hatred, self-righteous pride, and indignant judgment, will never foster hope and love, or change the hearts of others. In fact, it can do the opposite. It can spread the lie that Our Lord and Savior is not forgiving. It can spread the lie that Christ condemns and abhors those who have committed this sin, and that they cannot be forgiven. It can drive people away from the truth, back into Satan's captivity.

Hope is a delicate thing, and sharing it with those who need it is an act of love, one that heals and destroys despair. We can share hope by pointing out the falsity of the lies women believe.

We can spread hope by offering solutions to a woman's tangible problems, such as connecting her to services, providing for her needs, or sharing our own stories of redemption and forgiveness. Hope needs only to be a small flame in a dark room, just enough to see that the darkness won't last forever.

If we do not interact with abortion-advocating individuals in accordance with the Holy Spirit and with the theological virtues of faith, hope, and love, we do not act according to the model of Christ Jesus. All those in crisis pregnancies or those traumatized by abortion deserve hope, and what a blessed gift it is for those who offer it to them.

If God can take a man such as Saul of Tarsus and transform him into Paul the Apostle (Acts 9), why then should we not have hope in God's transforming powers for those who do evil and kill innocent life? Or for those who despair?

In March 2012, just three months after my parents had told me, "No, you can't come home," my mom flew to Texas, helped me pack up all my belongings, and drove me home. My parents always wanted the best for me. They were facing an unknown and scary situation, just like I was. They didn't know if "tough love" was the right thing, or if it would be better to support me and my unborn child physically and financially. In the end, compassion, love, and hope won out, and I gave birth to my daughter with my mom holding my hand, in the hospital fifteen minutes from home, not thousands of miles away and alone. We lived together for two years, and their support allowed me to go back to school and earn a teaching degree. Being together healed many wounds, fostered deep trust, and let hope flourish.

REFLECTION

What is it like to live without hope? Read the following Bible passages and imagine living in a world where hope was lost to you. Write down how you would feel.

We do not want you to be unaware, brothers, about those who have fallen asleep, so that you may not grieve like the rest, who have no hope. (1 Thessalonians 4:13)

My days are swifter than a weaver's shuttle;
  they come to an end without hope.
Remember that my life is like the wind;
  my eye will not see happiness again. (Job 7:6–7)

Therefore, remember that at one time you, Gentiles in the flesh, called the uncircumcision by those called the circumcision, which is done in the flesh by human hands, were at that time without Christ, alienated from the community of Israel and strangers to the covenants of promise, without hope and without God in the world. (Ephesians 2:11–12)

Have you ever felt despair or abandonment? What gave you hope? Who helped you to find and hold onto the hope that sustained you through your difficulty?

_____

_____

_____

_____

_____

_____

_____

Read Job 11:13–19 below. How does hope transform Job? How can it transform you? How can it transform those enslaved to abortion?

> If you set your heart aright
>   and stretch out your hands toward him,
> If iniquity is in your hand, remove it,
>   and do not let injustice dwell in your tent,
> Surely then you may lift up your face in innocence;
>   you may stand firm and unafraid.
> For then you shall forget your misery,
>   like water that has ebbed away you shall regard it.
> Then your life shall be brighter than the noonday;
>   its gloom shall become like the morning,
> And you shall be secure, because there is hope;
>   you shall look round you and lie down in safety;
> you shall lie down and no one will disturb you.

_____

_____

_____

_____

_____

_____

Of what use is hope during times of suffering? How can we encourage those in crisis pregnancy situations, or suffering after an abortion, to find hope? Think of tangible items, organizations in your community, words of encouragement, or things you can offer. Make a list.

_____

_____

_____

_____

_____

_____

_____

FIFTEEN

The Voice of the Post-Abortive Woman

It is to those who have the most need of us that
we ought to show our love more especially.
— St. Francis de Sales

The day I decided to step out of the darkness and admit I'd had an abortion was life-changing. I was pregnant with my son, my third crisis pregnancy, and I was ready for my life to change. Something had to give, and I was ready to lay down my lifestyle of selfishness and refocus on God. I longed to return to him. So, I loaded up my daughter and headed into town to the church where I was baptized, ready to receive the Sacrament of Reconciliation.

A thousand questions, insecurities, and lies rushed through my thoughts as I drove to the church, sat in the parking lot, and then made my way into the chapel. *You shouldn't go. It's too far. You can't let go of this secret! You have held it so long, it's a part of you now! Don't go! The priest will know you are a sinner! You can never be forgiven for what you did! Do you even have the strength to do this? Who do you think you are? You will never be able to hide from this! Once you open this door, you can never, ever close it!*

Finally, I entered the little confessional and sat face to face with the priest. He sounded calm. It was a calm I desperately needed. The storm inside my soul was crashing and churning, and I wanted to scream out this secret and let it go! I couldn't hold on anymore.

The priest began with the usual words, but I had no idea how to answer them. So instead, I said, "I don't even know what to say. I'm so sorry."

He didn't seem surprised, but he could tell that I was coming home to the Church after a long time away. He looked at me, straight at me. He saw me. The real me. The me that was still in there somewhere, hiding, searching for truth.

"Why don't you tell me why you are here?"

So I did. I told him about the abortion, about the mistakes I had made since then. I told him I had a child, and how her father abandoned me. I told him I was pregnant again, and the father was not present. I told him that I just wanted to start over, be done with this life of secrecy and sin.

"I'm so done!" I cried. "I'm so ready to be done with all this!"

"Do you know an act of contrition?" He asked me after listening. In the Catholic Church, an act of contrition is a prayer one says at the end of a confession asking for forgiveness and repenting of the sins committed.

I shook my head. The only prayers I had ever memorized were the Our Father and the Hail Mary.

"That's OK. I can see that you are sorry. Why don't you just tell God what you are sorry for, and repent in your own words."

The words flooded out of my body. Tears slid down my face so quickly, they ran over my chin and onto my neck. I sat on that chair, looking up to heaven, praying and pouring out the sin and the secret that had bound me for so many years. I begged the Lord to forgive me for murdering my son, for lacking courage, for lacking faith, for lying about it, for refusing to seek forgiveness, and for allowing fear to steal my child from me. I begged forgiveness for the sexual immorality that I had allowed to entrap and enslave me. And I begged for courage and love.

When the confession was over, I felt — for the first time in so many years — clean, bright air around me. I wiped those tears from my face, stood up, picked up my daughter, said, "Thank you, Father," and walked out of the room into a new life.

My story is not radical. It is not different, new, profound, or extreme. It is just one story of forgiveness, repentance, and new life. One example of what can happen for everyone who asks for forgiveness.

I often feel a connection with Saint Paul. He was a murderer, too. The story of Saul's conversion into the apostle Paul is beautiful, powerful, and encouraging. Acts 9 shares the story of Saul's conversion from a murderous zealot, conspiring to weed out Christians and bring them back to Jerusalem in chains to murder them, into a baptized Christian honoring Jesus Christ.

To read the story of Saul and his conversion, see Acts 7:54–60, Acts 9:1–30, and Acts 22:1–30.

The journey from murderous zealot to faithful servant of Christ was difficult and dangerous. Paul was persecuted by the Jews who had once honored him for his persecution of Christians. Jews and Gentiles both made plots to harm and kill Paul, for neither group believed or trusted him. Christians were suspicious of his transformation, and they did not believe that he was an apostle. After all, how could a treacherous man who held the cloaks of those stoning Stephen, the Christian martyr, truly change his heart? How could a man who went door to door, dragging men and women out of their homes and imprisoning them, truly change his heart? How could a man who voted for death when prisoners came before him for judgment truly change his heart?

Despite the challenges, Paul persisted on the path of righteousness and dedicated his life to Christ. His courage, fortitude, and virtue were aided by the Holy Spirit. Ultimately, he was imprisoned and put to death.

The voice of a woman who has had an abortion and turned to God is powerful. She is like Paul in so many ways. She and Paul both live with a murderous past. She who speaks against the abortion culture is called mad or crazy and is made to defend herself for her change of heart. Paul was told he was out of his mind and insane in Acts 26:24–25. Paul was forced to defend himself after his transformation as well. The post-abortive woman faces not only those in the abortion industry and the abortion-minded population who calls her a fraud and hates her for abandoning their side, but also faces a pro-life community who distrusts her and judges her for her past transgressions. After all, how could a woman who murders her own children ever be trusted? How could she ever truly be sorry and repent for her actions? There are always those among the pro-life community who are ready to remind her of what she has done, to heap hatred upon her, their anger at her actions never ceasing. For her, they have no compassion, no forgiveness, no love.

So, pro-lifers speak ill of her, and plot against her, and whisper curses at her behind closed doors. They shout, "Murderer!" at her and call her evil. They wish hell upon her and tell her over and over that she must repent — even if she has. Many want her to be punished with imprisonment or even death. They tell her she should feel grateful she is a free woman and not locked away where she belongs. They make an enemy of her, even while she stands between them and the culture of death. Despite their hostility, she holds her head high, saying, "Abortion is murder. I know. I murdered my child. Let me show you a better way."

Her voice is powerful beyond measure because, despite having enemies on both sides, she speaks the truth, bares her sin for all to see, and diligently tries to shield others and bring them out of the captivity of the evil of abortion. We must be careful that our words do not discourage her or send her back into captivity — back to silence or hopelessness that makes her incapable of speaking the truth.

Remember, too, that there are thousands of women who have had abortions who may not yet bear fruit, *but who still could*. And for this reason, we need to be sure that when we speak to or about women who have had abortions, we do not do so with hatred in our hearts.

In May 2018, Pope Francis approved a revision to the *Catechism* specifically stating that "the death penalty is inadmissible because it is an attack on the inviolability and dignity of the person" (2267). If any Catholic wishes death on a woman who has had an abortion, he or she is in direct contradiction to the teachings of the Church.

What purpose does it serve to send or post hurtful, angry, hateful messages online while we sit safely behind our keyboards typing, "Abortion is murder! You are a murderer!"

Where is the gentleness when we scream, "These women should be punished! Sent to prison for life! Given the death penalty!"

Where is the faithfulness when we condemn post-abortive mothers to hell in our own hearts and minds and give up the hope that the same Christ who redeemed Saul of Tarsus can redeem even the most enslaved woman?

Where is our self-control when we allow our anger and hatred to grow instead of fostering forgiveness?

Where is the kindness when we fail to defend these brave women who stand in the gap amidst a culture of death with enemies on both sides?

Where is the love and forbearance when we foster hatred in our hearts for the people enslaved by Satan's lies, captives in the horrible prison of the abortion industry and its ideology?

Let us never give Satan power over our words. Let us never offer him any seeds of hatred. Let us never yield the fruits of the Spirit to him, or forfeit the hope, faith, and love that was given to us in baptism. The next time you use your words, do so only with the armor of God firmly equipping you, and choose words that will help, not hinder God's work.

REFLECTION

The poem below describes emotional shock. How does this relate to our interactions with post-abortive mothers?

If shock is insufficient blood flow
through the human body,
then emotional shock
is insufficient love flow
through the heart and soul.

_____

_____

_____

_____

Read the Bible passage below. How can we protect ourselves from fostering hatred in our hearts?

Finally, draw your strength from the Lord and from his mighty power. Put on the armor of God so that you may be able to stand firm against the tactics of the devil. For our struggle is not with flesh and blood but with the principalities, with the powers, with the world rulers of this present darkness, with the evil spirits in the heavens. Therefore, put on the armor of God, that you may be able to resist on the evil day and, having done everything, to hold your ground. So stand fast with your loins girded in truth, clothed with righteousness as a breastplate, and your feet shod in readiness for the gospel of peace. In all circumstances, hold faith as a shield, to quench all [the] flaming arrows of the evil one. And take the helmet of salvation and the sword of the Spirit, which is the word of God. (Ephesians 6:10–17)

_____

_____

_____

_____

_____

_____

_____

Read the passages below. According to the passages, where does God put our sins after we have reconciled to him and been forgiven?

> Peace in place of bitterness!
> You have preserved my life
>   from the pit of destruction;
> Behind your back
>   you cast all my sins. (Isaiah 38:17)

> Will [you] again have compassion on us;
>   treading underfoot our iniquities?
> You will cast into the depths of the sea all our sins. (Micah 7:19)

> As far as the east is from the west,
> so far has he removed our sins from us. (Psalm 103:12)

_____

_____

_____

_____

_____

_____

_____

Read the passages below. According to the passages, how are we meant to interact with one another, especially those who have recognized their wrongs?

> Strive for peace with everyone, and for that holiness without which no one will see the Lord. (Hebrews 12:14)

> All bitterness, fury, anger, shouting, and reviling must be removed from you, along with all malice. [And] be kind to one another, compassionate, forgiving one another as God has forgiven you in Christ. (Ephesians 4:31–32)

> Put on then, as God's chosen ones, holy and beloved, heartfelt compassion, kindness, humility, gentleness, and patience, bearing with one another and forgiving one another, if one has a grievance against another; as the Lord has forgiven you, so must you also do. And over all these put on love, that is, the bond of perfection. And let the peace of Christ control your hearts, the peace into which you were also called in one body. And be thankful. (Colossians 3:12–15)

Research a story of a post-abortive woman. You may find stories on websites such as www.SilentNoMoreAwareness.org, or read Sheila Harper's abortion story in her book *Survivor: A Journey Through Abortion*, or search for my abortion story online at www .ElizabethGilletteAuthor.com. How does the firsthand account of abortion help soften your heart toward those who have suffered at the hands of the industry?

SIXTEEN

On Offenses against the Truth and Harming Others with Judgment

If something uncharitable is said in your presence, either speak in favor of the absent, or withdraw, or if possible, stop the conversation.
— St. John Vianney

Being the victim of gossip and rumors is incredibly painful, but perpetrating gossip and rumors is even worse. I have been both a victim and a perpetrator of gossip, rumors, rash judgment, calumny, and detraction. At first, speaking ill of others made me feel powerful. It allowed me to forget that I was an imperfect human by focusing on the wrongs and faults inside anyone but myself. In a way, it was a coping mechanism, but it quickly grew into a poisonous character fault that hurt not only those whom I targeted, but everyone who listened, and especially my own soul.

When others do not act in accordance with God's will, it can be easy to speak out against them in a way that fails to reflect their human dignity. The *Catechism* lists three sins that are offenses against truth, each very likely to cause unjust injury to another: rash judgment, detraction, and calumny (CCC 2477). The *Catechism* also forbids adulation, which is the act of encouraging or condoning another person's sin (CCC 2480).

Rash judgment is the act of assuming someone else has committed a sin or moral fault without a sufficient foundation to believe so. Pro-life individuals make thousands of rash judgments every day. Sometimes, we assume a woman who has had an abortion is not yet forgiven by Christ, and we direct her in an uncharitable way to repent. This diminishes the hope she has in her Savior and, if she has already repented, plants doubt that Christ has forgiven her after all. Rash judgment can be as dark as cursing another human being to hell, or as simple as assuming that every person who goes to an abortion facility is there for an abortion and then cultivating anger toward them in our hearts. In reality, perhaps one entered the facility as a contracted employee for a cleaning service, one was a delivery courier, and another was bringing her sister a medication she forgot at home but was crying in her car about her sister's choice. All of these rash judgments do more to destroy the truth in Christ than to advance his will. They do no good, and harm ourselves and others.

Detraction is the act of revealing another person's real faults to a third person without a valid reason to do so. *Calumny* is the act of making false statements that destroy a person's character. Calumny can be intentional or unintentional, as in statements that have no truth but are the result of gossip or judgment. The *Catechism* states: "Honor is the social witness given to human dignity, and everyone enjoys a natural right to the honor of his name and reputation and to respect. Thus, detraction and calumny offend against the virtues of justice and charity" (CCC 2479).

Every human being, whether participating in grave evil or not, has a natural right to human dignity, the honor of his name, his reputation, and respect. Therefore, we must always guard our thoughts and our words against criticizing another, especially if our motivation to do so is not charitable or lacks a clear purpose.

But what if the other person continues to participate in evil, or is not sorry for her sins? We still should not detract from her God-given human dignity because we do not know what the Holy Spirit is doing within her heart. If we detract from her dignity, we may be stunting the work of Christ within her. It is never necessary to gossip about a person or detract from a person's reputation or dignity. Never.

We should not lay out a person's moral faults for all to see, but we should also never condone the sins of another human being, no matter how big or how small they are. The *Catechism* also says:

> Every word or attitude is forbidden which by *flattery*, *adulation*, or *complaisance* encourages and confirms another in malicious acts and perverse conduct. Adulation is a grave fault if it makes one an accomplice in another's vices or grave sins. Neither the desire to be of service nor friendship justifies duplicitous speech. Adulation is a venial sin when it only seeks to be agreeable, to avoid

evil, to meet a need, or to obtain legitimate advantages."
(2480)

If we unpack this heavy paragraph, we learn that we should never praise or flatter another's flaws or sins — not even to protect a friendship, avoid evil, or obtain legitimate advantages. Likewise, we should never encourage someone in their sin. In the world of abortion, this obviously means that we should never condone or pay for an abortion or in any other way overlook or tolerate the death of innocent human life in the womb. We also can't excuse or overlook abortion in conversation or non-verbal communication. This means if someone approaches us about their abortion, we must not say anything or behave in any way that communicates that it is an acceptable choice.

So how do we avoid rash judgment, detraction, and calumny and still uphold the human dignity of every individual without falling to the sin of adulation?

In other words, how do we stand firm against the evils of abortion without harming our own souls or the souls of others through our thoughts and words? How do we tell the truth to those who need to hear it without destroying their dignity and hope?

St. Ignatius of Loyola wrote, "Every good Christian ought to be more ready to give a favorable interpretation to another's statement than to condemn it. But if he cannot do so, let him ask how the other understands it. And if the latter understands it badly, let the former correct him with love. If that does not suffice, let the Christian try all suitable ways to bring the other to a correct interpretation so that he may be saved."

Saint Ignatius instructs us to have an open dialogue "with love." He says we should "try all suitable ways to bring the other to a correct interpretation that he may be saved." But what is suitable?

"Your every act should be done with love" (1 Cor 16:14). What is love?

> Love is patient, love is kind. It is not jealous, [love] is not pompous, it is not inflated, it is not rude, it does not seek its own interests, it is not quick-tempered, it does not brood over injury, it does not rejoice over wrongdoing but rejoices with the truth. It bears all things, believes all things, hopes all things, endures all things. Love never fails. (1 Corinthians 13:4–8)

How difficult it is to actually interact at all times in accordance with the precept of love as described by Paul in his Letter to the Corinthians! One must be patient and kind. Slow to anger. Forgetful of wrongs. Rejoicing in the truth. Always protecting, trusting, hoping, and persevering. Paul promises that love never fails.

REFLECTION

What do these verses teach us about correcting someone who is sinning or in error?

> Brothers, even if a person is caught in some transgression, you who are spiritual should correct that one in a gentle spirit, looking to yourself, so that you also may not be tempted. (Galatians 6:1)

> Conduct yourselves wisely toward outsiders, making the most of the opportunity. Let your speech always be gracious, seasoned with salt, so that you know how you should respond to each one. (Colossians 4:5–6)

A mild answer turns back wrath,
  but a harsh word stirs up anger.
The tongue of the wise pours out knowledge,
  but the mouth of fool spews folly.
A soothing tongue is a tree of life,
  but a perverse one breaks the spirit. (Proverbs 15:1–2, 4)

No foul language should come out of your mouths, but only such as is good for needed edification, that it may impart grace to those who hear. [And] be kind to one another, compassionate, forgiving one another as God has forgiven you in Christ. (Ephesians 4:29, 32)

If your brother sins [against you], go and tell him his fault between you and him alone. If he listens to you, you have won over your brother. If he does not listen, take one or two others along with you, so that "every fact may be established on the testimony of two or three witnesses." If he refuses to listen to them, tell the church. If he refuses to listen even to the church, then treat him as you would a Gentile or a tax collector. (Matthew 18:15–17)

_____

_____

Have you ever found yourself in a situation where you were tempted to sin through rash judgment, detraction, calumny, or adulation? What can you do or say to avoid falling into these sins again?

_____

_____

_____

_____

_____

_____

_____

During his Wednesday audience on September 25, 2019, Pope Francis said, "We know that calumny always kills. This 'diabolical cancer' of calumny — born from a desire to destroy a person's reputation — also assaults the rest of the ecclesial body and seriously damages it when, for petty interests or to cover their own faults, (people) unite to sully someone." How does calumny act like cancer? And how can it affect your pro-life work?

_____

_____

_____

_____

_____

_____

_____

_____

In the event that a conversation devolves into one of rash judgment, detraction, calumny, or adulation, how might you need to interact differently with a fellow follower of Christ as opposed to someone who does not yet know Christ?

_____

_____

_____

_____

_____

_____

_____

SEVENTEEN

Divisions Among Us

Division comes from the Devil.
— Pope Francis

Shortly after I returned to the Church following my reconciliation, I began seeing a counselor and made an enormous amount of progress toward healing emotionally and mentally. I loved my counseling sessions, I stopped having nightmares, and I was making amazing progress in a one-on-one setting with my very compassionate secular counselor.

Then, one evening, I was approached by a woman representing a post-abortion recovery retreat. She offered me the opportunity to attend, saying it was necessary to heal from my abortion. She truly believed that it would be impossible for me to heal without attending this particular retreat.

Over the years, I have been approached by several other individuals who likewise said that I couldn't find healing unless I participated in a healing retreat. While I am sure they intended to help, they didn't realize that I was already well on my way to healing, and the path that I chose was the right path for me as an individual. Following my abortion, I developed post-traumatic stress disorder and an eating disorder that needed to be treated by a trained professional, in conjunction with my emotional pain, nightmares, guilt, and sadness stemming from my abortion.

The idea that there is only one way to heal is born out of pride. When we begin to offer our own group, book, idea, opinion, retreat, and the like as the only way, or as the best option, we dismiss the plethora of other beautiful connections and resources the pro-life ministry offers. We isolate ourselves and create divisions.

For pro-life advocates, unity is essential. There are hundreds of thousands of individuals who stand up to defend the lives of innocent children in the womb, and that means there are hundreds of thousands of individual people with their own thoughts, words, deeds, and actions, each with separate motivations, goals, and outcomes.

Divisions are nothing new to the faithful. Jesus warned about division in his Church (see Mt 12:25). The disciples discussed this problem among themselves often. Divisions popped up all around them. Heresies took shape, and the followers of Christ began to be deceived, torn apart from one another, and dispersed. They quarreled about genealogies, the law, and other unimportant things (Ti 3:9). Today, we continue to suffer from divisions within the Body of Christ. Political divisions abound, as do divisions regarding social justice issues, money, and scandals. They all hinder the unity of Christians. Saint Paul urged Christians to "watch out for those who create dissensions and obstacles ... avoid them" (Rom 16:17).

Among those who fight for the unborn and those affected by abortion, it is important to always be vigilant to protect the work we do together and avoid foolish quarreling that does not advance the Lord's will that all should have life.

There are many divisions among us. There are those who say abortion is acceptable in instances of rape or if the child is deformed or terminally ill. There are those who say the best way to stop a woman from entering an abortion clinic is by displaying large, graphic images of aborted children so as to shock her away from her appointment. Others say that women who have had abortions should be imprisoned as an example to future generations of women. Still others condone violence against abortion clinics, doctors, and workers, although this is extremely rare.

There are thousands of nonprofit organizations, Bible study groups, churches, and individuals working tirelessly in their own niches. Often, they don't know about each other, or if they do, they don't know how to work together. In some cases, they don't want to work together, because doing so might damage their own pride, popularity, or financial success.

But there is hope. The *Catechism* describes believers who respond to God's word as members of Christ's Body. The Body's unity does not make the diversity of its members disappear. Rather, the Spirit of God who is within us gives each of us unique gifts for the welfare of the Church. The diversity of the members of Christ's Body is necessary and beautiful. It is the unity of this Mystical Body that triumphs over all human divisions (791).

It is good that we have many missions, many groups, many nonprofits, many authors, many prayer warriors, many languages, and so forth. These are beautiful gifts that we have been given to help us. They allow each of us to participate in God's mission and advance it. They also help us reach many different people.

Our challenge as members of Christ's Body is to work together, not to remain divided. We can and should share our own gifts, never worrying about who has more, who does more, or who receives more in return. By working together, sharing with each other, and helping one another, we will reach our goal without distractions or division.

Working together may look different for each group. Some examples include: sharing contact information for a local pregnancy clinic with women in crisis; giving a man whose child was aborted information for a men's post-abortion recovery group; sending a post-abortive woman to an organization other than your own, if you realize she will receive more care there than you can offer; donating money to a group that can reach people you cannot reach; reading books, blogs, websites, and watching media from other ministry groups; praying for one another daily; and making friends and keeping in contact with people from other groups as you work in your various ministries, so that you can encourage each other.

REFLECTION

According to these Scriptures, what do we need to be wary of when we work in the pro-life ministry?

For you are still of the flesh. While there is jealousy and rivalry among you, are you not of the flesh, and behaving in an ordinary human way? (1 Corinthians 3:3)

Avoid foolish arguments, genealogies, rivalries, and quarrels about the law, for they are useless and futile. (Titus 3:9)

I urge you, brothers, to watch out for those who create

dissensions and obstacles, in opposition to the teaching that you learned; avoid them. For such people do not serve our Lord Christ but their own appetites, and by fair and flattering speech they deceive the hearts of the innocent. (Romans 16:17–18)

I urge you, brothers, in the name of our Lord Jesus Christ, that all of you agree in what you say, and that there be no divisions among you, but that you be united in the same mind and in the same purpose. (1 Corinthians 1:10)

_____

_____

_____

_____

_____

_____

_____

We cannot face a world divided with a mission divided. If Satan has any foothold among us, we struggle. Read the following Scripture and think about what we can do as a pro-life community to become a "strong man."

Summoning them, he began to speak to them in parables. "How can Satan drive out Satan? If a kingdom is divided against itself, that kingdom cannot stand. And if a house is divided against itself, that house will not be able to stand. And if Satan has risen up against himself and is divided, he cannot stand; that is the end of him. But no one can enter a strong man's house to plunder his property unless he first ties up the strong man. Then he can plunder his house. (Mark 3:23–27)

According to the following verse, who causes divisions? What should we do to build ourselves up in faith?

But you, beloved, remember the words spoken before-hand by the apostles of our Lord Jesus Christ, for they told you, "In [the] last time there will be scoffers who will live according to their own godless desires." These are the ones who cause divisions; they live on the natural plane, devoid of the Spirit. But you, beloved, build yourselves up in your most holy faith; pray in the holy Spirit. Keep yourselves in the love of God and wait for the mercy of our Lord Jesus Christ that leads to eternal life. On those who waver, have mercy; save others by snatching them out of the fire; on others have mercy with fear, abhorring even the outer garment stained by the flesh. (Jude 1:17–23)

_____

_____

What can you do to ensure the pro-life ministries near you work together and do not become divided?

_____

_____

_____

_____

_____

_____

_____

_____

EIGHTEEN

Above All, Love

What we do is but one drop in the ocean. But
by not doing it, the ocean is one drop less.
— St. Teresa of Calcutta

Many people wonder what they should do to help the pro-life ministry. Attend a march? Start a group at church? Pray outside an abortion facility? The answer is different for each of us, but there is one thing we all should do, beginning this very moment: We must love.

"We love because he first loved us" (1 Jn 4:19). Love is a verb. It is a choice and an action. It means setting aside our shortcomings, our judgments, our anger, and any other barriers between ourselves and God's will. It must begin with us. The change we make in our own hearts and souls will spread outward as an example for those around us. Our love will light a fire that cannot be extinguished.

If you are ready to begin or expand your pro-life ministry, reach out to those in your community who are already active. Your church may have a pro-life committee. If your church does not, other local parishes or churches in your community may. Reach out to local crisis pregnancy resource centers and ask them what their immediate needs are. Reflect on your own talents and gifts, and consider offering them to those running the pregnancy resource centers. Perhaps they need more funding. Can you organize a fundraiser at your church or in your community? Perhaps they need to spruce up their office. Can you paint, decorate, or donate time organizing clothing and diapers?

Ask the local private or public schools if they have a club such as Students for Life. Is there a club at your local community college or university? Is there interest in starting one?

Subscribe to your local or state Right to Life emails and newsletters. Contact your diocese and inquire about their programs, activities, and involvement. Ask what their immediate needs are, and offer your talents, gifts, and expertise.

Consider becoming trained as a Sidewalk Advocate for Life, or join a group of people who pray outside your local abortion clinics.

If you feel called to minister to those men and women who have had abortions, research the available abortion healing groups such as Rachel's Vineyard or Save One. Inquire about bringing a healing group to your parish, helping to put on a retreat, or simply praying fervently for those attending. Mark your calendar for upcoming retreats and groups meeting in your area, and commit to praying for them, by name if possible.

Create an address book with your community and state pro-life contacts. As you immerse yourself in activities and events, you will network with passionate people. Keeping their contact information in one place will ensure you can stay connected with them and stay informed when activities arise.

Join a Life Chain event or a 40 Days for Life campaign. Praying is powerful, essential, and accessible to everyone.

Write encouraging letters to those already active in the ministry.

If you are inclined, get involved in your local or state politics. It is possible that individuals or groups have already or are currently drafting bills to make lasting change in government. Joining a campaign for a pro-life measure is a way to make a difference.

If you are financially able, purchase diapers every time you go to the grocery store, even if you don't have a baby. Donate them to your local pregnancy resource center, or to someone in your community who is struggling.

No matter what you choose to do in your personal ministry, be brave. Do not fear the unknown or the enemy. Do not fear the growing pains that come with changing our own hearts. Do not fear failure, or spiritual or physical attacks. Do not despair but have hope that God is in control (see Romans 8:28).

Above all, love.

REFLECTION

Read the following Bible passages and be encouraged. Meditate on them and write down any encouragement the Holy Spirit gives you.

> For you did not receive a spirit of slavery to fall back into fear, but you received a spirit of adoption, through which we cry, "Abba, Father!" (Romans 8:15)

There is no fear in love, but perfect love drives out fear because fear has to do with punishment, and so one who fears is not yet perfect in love. (1 John 4:18)

I command you: be strong and steadfast! Do not fear nor be dismayed, for the LORD, your God, is with you wherever you go. (Joshua 1:9)

Even though I walk through the valley of the shadow of
     death,
  I will fear no evil, for you are with me;
  your rod and your staff comfort me. (Psalm 23:4)

Throughout this book, you have studied a perspective not often explored in the pro-life ministry: one of self-examination and interior growth. Read the passage below. What have you learned during this process? How has it renewed your soul or your relationship with Christ?

Therefore, we are not discouraged; rather, although our

outer self is wasting away, our inner self is being renewed day by day. For this momentary light affliction
is producing for us an eternal weight of glory beyond all
comparison, as we look not to what is seen but to what is
unseen; for what is seen is transitory, but what is unseen
is eternal. (2 Corinthians 4:16–18)

In a journal, write a prayer asking Christ to be with you, to guide
you as you continue your journey in the pro-life ministry. You
may wish to ask him to point out any shortcomings you may
have. You may wish to give thanks for all that you have learned
and the gifts he has given you to help you continue to say yes to
his will, his ministry, and his work.

_____

_____

_____

_____

Brainstorm and write a list of things you can do to start or expand your ministry. Which of these things can you realistically do immediately? Which of them can you research more? Which of them do you want to consider in the future?

_____

_____

_____

_____

_____

_____

_____

Examination of Conscience

Be ashamed when you sin, not when you repent.
— St. John Chrysostom

The examination of conscience is a prayerful self-reflection on our words and deeds in the light of the Gospel. It can help us determine how we may have sinned against God. We should prepare for the Sacrament of Penance by first completing a thorough examination. The *Catechism* states that "the reception of [the Sacrament of Reconciliation] ought to be prepared for by an *examination of conscience* made in the light of the Word of God. The passages best suited to this can be found in the Ten Commandments, the moral catechesis of the Gospels and the

155

apostolic Letters, such as the Sermon on the Mount and the apostolic teachings" (1454).

The following examination will help you delve deep into your own conscience and your pro-life ministry.

Find a quiet place where you can think, pray, and study. Read each question slowly, and think about your actions, words, thoughts, and deeds. Some find it helpful to write their answers on paper to take to the Sacrament of Reconciliation. You can destroy the paper after your confession, for your sins are as far as the east is from the west! (see Ps 103:12).

Have I had an abortion, paid for another's abortion, encouraged someone to have an abortion, or in any way helped another individual have an abortion?

Have I lost faith in God, in his love for me and others, or in what he can accomplish?

Have I been angry or sown hatred toward those who have had abortions or those who advocate for abortions?

Have I devalued the dignity of another human through deeds, actions, thoughts, or spoken or written words?

Have I wished death or harm to another person?

Have I desired revenge against another person?

Have I desired harsh judgment, such as life imprisonment for a post-abortive mother, abortion providers, or workers?

Have I provoked another to anger or hatred through my words, actions, or attitudes?

Have I cursed another human with my words or thoughts?

Have my words contributed to the death of another person, either spiritually or physically?

Have I had an unbridled tongue and spoken words that harmed another?

Have I admonished another without love and care, or to elevate myself in a self-righteous manner?

Have I wished those entrenched in the culture of abortion would be sterilized or unable to bear children?

Have I contributed to division, dissension, or the destruction of peace with my words, thoughts, actions, or deeds?

Have I committed detraction by revealing the moral faults or sins of another person?

Have I sinned against another or against God through lies, exaggeration, or any form of falsehood?

Have I diminished the hope of another person through my actions, words, or attitudes?

Have I contributed to the despair of another person through my actions, words, or attitudes?

Have I been unnecessarily argumentative?

Have I refused to forgive another person?

Have I brought up the sins and transgressions of another person even after they were forgiven by God?

Have I judged another person rashly or wrongfully, or interpreted their words, thoughts, or actions in an unfavorable way?

Have I disrespected the reputation of another person?

Have I encouraged or condoned the sin of another person by means of adulation or complacence?

Have I boasted or bragged about myself?

Have I maliciously caricatured some aspect of another person's behavior?

Have I attributed malice to another person's actions or words instead of receiving them with charity?

Have I attempted to make things right after harming the reputation or dignity of another person?

Have I used social communication platforms in an unloving way?

Have I scandalized those around me or those in my care by leading them to sin or by giving in to sin through vices, deeds, or omissions?

Have I scandalized those who are in a weak position emotionally, financially, or physically? Have I provoked them to anger, manipulated them to turn away from their moral values, or otherwise corrupted their religious practice?

Have I used my power in such a way as to lead others to do wrong?

Have I contributed to or created divisions in my ministry?

Have I been prideful with regard to my work in the pro-life ministry?

Have I given of myself in service with resentment, envy, or pride?

Have I sought fame or self-gratification in my ministry?

Have I purposefully withheld the knowledge of available pro-life organizations or help from someone in need?

Have I been lazy in my assigned duties, or the duties for which I volunteered?

Have I failed to pray or seek God's wisdom before engaging with others?

Have I failed to discern the needs of another in a particular moment?

Have I advocated for my own desires or opinions instead of God's will?

Prayers

The following prayers may give you comfort, strength, and protection as you journey through your ministry. May they help you embrace growth within and equip you for your mission, which is, above all, love.

THE PRAYER OF SAINT FRANCIS OF ASSISI

Lord, make me an instrument of your peace:
where there is hatred, let me sow love;
where there is injury, pardon;
where there is doubt, faith;
where there is despair, hope;
where there is darkness, light;
where there is sadness, joy.
O divine Master,
grant that I may not so much seek
to be consoled as to console,

to be understood as to understand,
to be loved as to love.
For it is in giving that we receive,
it is in pardoning that we are pardoned,
and it is in dying that we are born to eternal life.
Amen.
(a traditional prayer for peace, not written by St. Francis)

PRAYER TO ST. MICHAEL THE ARCHANGEL

St. Michael the Archangel, defend us in battle; be our defense against the wickedness and snares of the Devil. May God rebuke him, we humbly pray; and do thou, O prince of the heavenly host, by the power of God, thrust into hell Satan and the other evil spirits who prowl about the world seeking the ruin of souls. Amen.

POPE BENEDICT XVI'S PRAYER FOR THE UNBORN

Lord Jesus,
        You who faithfully visit and fulfill with your Presence the Church and the history of men;
        You who in the miraculous Sacrament of your Body and Blood render us participants in divine Life and allow us a foretaste of the joy of eternal Life;
We adore and bless you.
        Prostrated before You, source and lover of Life, truly present and alive among us, we beg you.
        Reawaken in us respect for every unborn life, make us capable of seeing in the fruit of the maternal womb the miraculous work of the Creator, open our hearts to generously welcoming every child that comes into life.
        Bless all families, sanctify the union of spouses, render fruitful their love.

Accompany the choices of legislative assemblies with the light of your Spirit, so that peoples and nations may recognize and respect the sacred nature of life, of every human life.

Guide the work of scientists and doctors, so that all progress contributes to the integral well-being of the person, and no one endures suppression or injustice.

Give creative charity to administrators and economists, so they may realize and promote sufficient conditions so that young families can serenely embrace the birth of new children.

Console the married couples who suffer because they are unable to have children
and in Your goodness provide for them.

Teach us all to care for orphaned or abandoned children, so they may experience the warmth of your Charity, the consolation of your divine Heart.

Together with Mary, Your Mother, the great believer, in whose womb you took on our human nature, we wait to receive from You, our Only True Good and Savior, the strength to love and serve life, in anticipation of living forever in You, in communion with the Blessed Trinity.

PRAYER FOR THE BEATITUDES

Lord,

I invite you into my life, and into my pro-life ministry.

You say that the poor in spirit are blessed, for theirs is the kingdom of heaven. Help me to recognize and embrace my own spiritual poverty and give me a strong desire to seek an unending, unwavering bond with you. Come to me and fill me with your presence, your grace, and your mercy. In my spiritual weakness, give me strength. Cultivate in me humility and a longing for you.

You say, blessed are they who mourn, for they will be comforted. Lord, open my heart, and break it for what breaks yours.

Help me to mourn those who are lost to abortion and those who are captives to the evils of abortion and the abortion culture. Help me to feel the sorrow, grief, and anguish of those who have been affected by abortion in any capacity. Mourn within me, O Lord, and comfort me and all those around me with the promise of your everlasting love and your victory over death.

You say that the meek are blessed, for they will inherit the land. Lord, I cannot be meek on my own, but you can cultivate it within me. Fill my heart with gentle tenderness, always speaking with love. Help me to embrace humility and set aside arrogance. Take control of my tongue, my thoughts, and my actions. Let all that I do, speak, and think be done in love. For it is the meek who will inherit the land, and the meek who are best suited to cultivate the human heart.

You say that they who hunger and thirst for righteousness are blessed, for they will be satisfied. Lord, cultivate in me a hunger and a thirst for righteousness and a zeal to protect the unborn and their mothers, and every human being who was created with dignity in your image and likeness. Do not let me grow weary of the fight or yield the hunger and thirst when the battle seems lost. Satisfy my hunger and my thirst, O Lord, with your victory over death and slavery to sin. Help me always to hunger and thirst for righteousness in a way that only demonstrates your love to the world. Remove from me anger, judgment, despair, hate, detraction, and dishonesty.

You say that the merciful are blessed, for they will be shown mercy. Plant in me a desire to be always merciful. Give me a deep compassion for all those whom you have created. Help me to see first their dignity, their humanity, their precious value. Help me to offer true forgiveness, kindness. Let every interaction I have with the world and those championing the culture of death be gentle, merciful, and loving. Help me to remember who the true enemy is.

You say that those with a clean heart are blessed, for they will see God. Lord, grant that I may look inward at my own short-comings and be convicted to lay them at your feet. Create in me a clean heart, so that I may cooperate with your will and never do harm to your purpose. Grant that when my time on earth has expired, I may see you in eternity.

You say that the peacemakers are blessed, for they will be called children of God. Help me to always calm the stormy waters and sow peace. Peace among believers, peace among those who do not know you, peace among those who mourn and are hopeless, peace among those who fight for death and those who long for life. Tame my tongue, my thoughts, my actions, and my deeds so that everything I do is done with love, and to cultivate, protect, and honor your peace. Lord, never let me sow dissension, anger, hate, or judgment. Let me be called a child of God.

You say that those who are persecuted for the sake of righteousness are blessed, for theirs is the kingdom of heaven. Protect me from falling into despair when the persecution cuts deep. Help me to stand firm in the truth, and not to fear the anger and hate that will swirl around me. Teach me to find joy in persecution, and to cooperate with the Holy Spirit so that even in the trials of persecution, you may be glorified, and souls may be saved from the horrible chains and bondage of abortion. Let me always offer my trials and pains to Jesus Christ, who was the first to be persecuted, and who was the first to triumph over it with love and self-sacrifice.

Lord, I invite you into my life, and into my pro-life ministry. Come, Holy Spirit, come, so that I may be all that I was created to be!

Amen.

PRAYER OF ST. BENEDICT

O Lord, I place myself in your hands and dedicate myself to you.

I pledge myself to do your will in all things: To love the Lord God with all my heart, all my soul, all my strength.

Not to kill. Not to steal. Not to covet. Not to bear false witness. To honor all persons. Not to do to another what I would not wish done to myself. To chastise the body. Not to seek after pleasures. To love fasting. To relieve the poor. To clothe the naked. To visit the sick. To bury the dead. To help in trouble. To console the sorrowing. To hold myself aloof from worldly ways. To prefer nothing to the love of Christ.

Not to give way to anger. Not to foster a desire for revenge. Not to entertain deceit in the heart. Not to make a false peace. Not to forsake charity. Not to swear, lest I swear falsely. To speak the truth with heart and tongue. Not to return evil for evil. To do no injury: yea, even to bear patiently any injury done to me. To love my enemies. Not to curse those who curse me, but rather to bless them. To bear persecution for justice's sake.

Not to be proud. Not to be given to intoxicating drink. Not to be an over-eater. Not to be lazy. Not to be slothful. Not to be a murmurer. Not to be a detractor. To put my trust in God.

To refer the good I see in myself to God. To refer any evil in myself to myself. To fear the Day of Judgment. To be in dread of hell. To desire eternal life with spiritual longing. To keep death before my eyes daily. To keep constant watch over my actions. To remember that God sees me everywhere. To call upon Christ for defense against evil thoughts that arise in my heart.

To guard my tongue against wicked speech. To avoid much speaking. To avoid idle talk. To read only what is good to read. To look at only what is good to see. To pray often. To ask forgiveness daily for my sins, and to seek ways to amend my life. To obey my superiors in all things rightful. Not to desire to be thought holy, but to seek holiness.

To fulfill the commandments of God by good works. To love chastity. To hate no one. Not to be jealous or envious of anyone.

Not to love strife. Not to love pride. To honor the aged. To pray for my enemies. To make peace after a quarrel, before the setting of the sun. Never to despair of your mercy, O God of Mercy. Amen.

LITANY OF HUMILITY

O Jesus! meek and humble of heart, hear me.
From the desire of being esteemed, deliver me, O Jesus.
From the desire of being loved, deliver me, O Jesus.
From the desire of being extolled, deliver me, O Jesus.
From the desire of being honored, deliver me, O Jesus.
From the desire of being praised, deliver me, O Jesus.
From the desire of being preferred to others, deliver me, O Jesus.
From the desire of being consulted, deliver me, O Jesus.
From the desire of being approved, deliver me, O Jesus.
From the fear of being humiliated, deliver me, O Jesus.
From the fear of being despised, deliver me, O Jesus.
From the fear of suffering rebukes, deliver me, O Jesus.
From the fear of being calumniated, deliver me, O Jesus.
From the fear of being forgotten, deliver me, O Jesus.
From the fear of being ridiculed, deliver me, O Jesus.
From the fear of being wronged, deliver me, O Jesus.
From the fear of being suspected, deliver me, O Jesus.
That others may be loved more than I, Jesus, grant me the grace to desire it.
That others may be esteemed more than I, Jesus, grant me the grace to desire it.
That, in the opinion of the world, others may increase and I may decrease, Jesus, grant me the grace to desire it.
That others may be chosen and I set aside, Jesus, grant me the grace to desire it.
That others may be praised and I unnoticed, Jesus, grant me the grace to desire it.

That others may be preferred to me in everything, Jesus, grant me the grace to desire it.

That others may become holier than I, provided that I may become as holy as I should, Jesus, grant me the grace to desire it.

About the Author

Like so many women, Elizabeth Gillette experienced abortion firsthand. The traumatic experience shook her faith, causing devastating side effects. Through the saving grace of Jesus Christ, she found healing and forgiveness, and began to speak out against the industry that nearly destroyed her. Her testimony has been shared in multiple court cases throughout the United States and featured on radio and TV broadcasts. Now, Elizabeth writes and speaks about how love conquers the greatest tragedy of our time, abortion. Elizabeth is the mother of four living children, and a passionate advocate for life.